Helping Youth Grieve

Helping Youth Grieve

The Good News of Biblical Lament

Bob Yoder

RESOURCE *Publications* · Eugene, Oregon

Resource Publications
An Imprint of Wipf and Stock Publishers
199 W. 8th Ave., Suite 3
Eugene, OR 97401

www.wipfandstock.com

ISBN 13: 978-1-4982-2042-2

Manufactured in the U.S.A.   04/06/2015

To Pamela,

your impeccable loving support of me through these years is indescribable. You have tolerated my rants, brainstorms, nonsensical thoughts, and joys in ways that demonstrate your character as one of emulating the steadfast love of God.

Thank you.

Psalm 13

How long, O Lord? Will you forget me forever?

How long will you hide your face from me?

How long must I bear pain in my soul, and have sorrow in my heart all day long?

How long shall my enemy be exalted over me?

Consider and answer me, O Lord my God!

Give light to my eyes, or I will sleep the sleep of death, and my enemy will say, "I have prevailed"; my foes will rejoice because I am shaken.

But I trusted in your steadfast love; my heart shall rejoice in your salvation.

I will sing to the Lord, because he has dealt bountifully with me.

Contents

Contents

Preface

IN RECENT DECADES THERE has been an increase in eating disorders, depression, suicide and other mental health illnesses among American adolescents. Youth are immersed in a world of pressures, pain, and loss. Yet our culture propagates a "feel good" attitude that denies constructive expressions of lament, but strives for high demands of success. Theologically, we have narrowed a view of God as a therapeutic being who "helps us" when we need to feel good. *Helping Youth Grieve* explores the role of biblical lament in the pastoral care and faith formation of early, middle, and late adolescents as a response to these cultural realities. This book overviews a theology of biblical lament and then suggests that adult spiritual caregivers practice lament with their young people by using a three-step, six-minute, timed-writing prayer exercise.

Acknowledgements

To my parents. You helped me know what unconditional love is. You taught me to be honest with God and modeled a faith that I now try to carry on with my own children.

To Dr. Jaco Hamman. Thank you for challenging me to go deeper and wider when the seeds of this book were germinating. Your insightful perspectives spurred on my passion to explore the complexities of ministry with people, particularly through the graceful act of lament and mourning our losses.

To Sarah, Daniel, Loanne, and Aaron. You graciously led your adolescent youth through four sessions of writing their own lament. Your help with the project is forever appreciated.

To Goshen College. Thank you for making an opportunity available to me to more thoroughly delve into the study of biblical lament, and pastoral care and faith formation of adolescents.

To the many people, youth and adults, who allowed me to lead them in practices of biblical lament. And, who offered constructive conversation in return.

To God. Thank you for giving me life, breath, a mind, and passion. I praise you for allowing me to be honest with you and for welcoming my rants, anger, and pain over the years. Your grace and steadfast love is to be exalted. Your Good News is to be praised.

1

Introduction

I WAS IN SEVENTH grade. My father and I were completing chores on our dairy farm when a car came speeding down our lane to let us know that my older brother was in a serious car accident not far from our home. I was stunned and not sure how to respond, but as my father drove my mother and me to the accident site I held back my tears, downplaying my emotions. However, these attempts were not successful as my father heard me sniffle. Rather than suggest that I "be a man" and hold in my tears, he simply said, "Bobby, it's okay to cry." In that moment my father gave me permission to express my feelings and fears.

My father modeled that type of emotional expression in other public venues. He led hymns in the churches we attended. Sometimes as he described the story behind the song, he would be overcome by the emotion of it and shed tears in public. Dad would often crack a joke about having too much farm dust in his eyes and that they "were in need of a good washing." He let his emotions show not to manipulate others, but because his genuine tears caught him off guard. As a child and early adolescent, my father modeled to me that it was indeed okay for men to cry and express their emotions.

A second personal story comes from my first year in college. During Spring Break my friend Jeff died unexpectedly due to an undiagnosed heart problem. We had grown up together and attended the same college. This was the first person close to me who ever died. I remember going to the funeral home expecting to be a source of support to my friends. Instead, I lost it when I approached the casket as the reality of his death sank into me. Lynn, who had been a volunteer youth worker while I was part of the church youth program, simply came and held me in his arms as I wept. That expression of care helped me to stay in the moment of accepting Jeff's death as I recalled many wonderful memories of him. I would look at Jeff's body and then bury my face into Lynn's arms and cry. Then I would look at the casket for a brief time and once again plunge my head into Lynn's comforting arms. This cycle went on for nearly twenty minutes. Throughout that entire time, I do not recall Lynn ever saying a word. Later when I became a pastor, I relied on that image of pastoral care as a comforting presence when I walked with people in their hurts and losses. Indeed, Lynn enabled me to face the reality of that significant loss and granted me permission to grieve from the depths of my soul.

Two Current Challenging Realities

1. What kind of humans are adolescents being formed into?

The previous stories are shaping moments from my youth, but I am not sure that today's youth have enough of those types of faith mentors for them to enter into their deep emotions and grieve their raw feelings. Compared to a few decades ago, adolescents today are more likely to commit suicide,[1] to suffer from mental heath illnesses such as depression and eating disorders and self-mutilation, and to live in a home whose parent has been remarried due to divorce. Adolescents today face pressures of "growing up" that were not present a few decades ago with the increase of technology and to a society that emphasizes success at an earlier age. Our American culture is one that busies and hurries our young

1. Centers for Disease Control and Prevention. "Suicide Among Youth," lines 1–3, 9.

people to unhealthy levels of stress and tiredness.[2] Even before our children have reached the onset of adolescence it seems they are "stressed out" due to responsibility, emotional, and information overloads.[3] Eighty percent of R-rated movies target underage children, 30 percent of music recordings with explicit content identify teenagers as the market, and 70 percent of "mature" video games are pitched to younger teens.[4] All of this is happening as they discover who they are and what they want to do in life while they also live through the developmental changes during junior high, senior high, and young adulthood.

Adolescence is a time when young people struggle for a sense of identity and belonging. Who will they be when they "grow up"? What vocation will they embrace? Whose influential voices will they claim as their loyalty? They will face much change in this relatively short span of years. Personal and societal pressures abound. I believe the statistics in the previous paragraph offer a glimpse of how some adolescents respond to the many pressures and realities they face. Overall, I believe that adult spiritual caregivers need to better prepare and enable young people to encounter all the significant losses they will experience in this relatively short period of time.

Chap Clark, author of *Hurt 2.0: Inside the World of Today's Teenagers*, argues that the defining issue for contemporary adolescents, particularly midadolescents, is abandonment.[5] He wrote this book hoping to convince people that life is different for high schoolers today compared to thirty years ago, or at any time in history, and that adults who walk with youth must wake up to this new reality. The adult world has systemically abandoned the youth of this generation from both external and internal systems.

Externally, the adult-driven institutions, including schools and churches, are primarily concerned with adult agendas, needs,

---

2. Clark, *Hurt 2.0*, 131–132.

3. Elkind, *The Hurried Child*, chapters 1 and 8.

4. Ibid., xi.

5. Clark, *Hurt 2.0*, 27.

and dreams.[6] In recent decades, our society has moved from "being a relatively stable and cohesive adult community intent on caring for the needs of the young to a free-for-all of independent and fragmented adults seeking their own survival . . . deepening a hole of systemic rejection."[7] Internally, adolescents have suffered from the loss of safe relationships and intimate settings, primarily due to the re-definement of "family" in our culture and an increased divorce rate.[8] There has been a shift in the past three decades from when the definition of family was accepted to be "two or more persons related by birth, marriage or adoption who reside in the same household to the current definition of a free-flowing, organic 'commitment' between people who love each other."[9]

Since youth are abandoned by the adult institutions in their lives, they are forced to deal with pain and fear on their own and therefore have created a "world beneath," a unique and defended social system. This world exists because they believe they have no choice and are searching for a relationally focused safe home to band together. However, in spite of all this and even though Clark ultimately found a greater chasm in his research between adults and youth than he anticipated, he still suggests that youth want adults and desire genuine, authentic relationships.

Whether or not one completely agrees with Clark's assessment of adolescent realities, his findings are provocative and should cause us to pause and reflect on the lives of the young people we know. It also seems that the influence of our success-oriented culture and its accompanying stresses has impacted our church ministries and adolescent spiritual caregiving practices. A culture of success offers praise for our accomplishments and denies or downplays our failures. Could it be that in the church we have over-emphasized praise to God to the neglect of truly facing our fears, our doubts, our pains, our struggles, and our weaknesses? Do we think that God does not appreciate those times of vulnerable

6. Ibid., 30.
7. Ibid., 15.
8. Ibid., 34–35.
9. Ibid., 16.

suffering because we believe this to be a sign of weak faith? In our gathered times of worship, do we over-engage in songs that offer praise to God and neglect truly facing our human frailties? Is such an imbalanced use of praise songs another symptom of an American society that demands success?

Personally, I appreciate and enjoy singing songs that offer praise to God; we can find many wonderful psalms of praise in the Bible. However, I am concerned that if an adolescent population only knows how to pray to God through the genre of praise, then it is in danger of neglecting other forms of biblical prayer, particularly when suicide, abuse, depression, eating disorders, cutting, and other adolescent expressions of a pain-filled life are on the rise. Can such people authentically offer praise to God if they have never first talked with God about their hurts, losses, and sufferings? Do we as adult spiritual caregivers contribute to some of the blame for such a one-sided view of spirituality? In other words, do we model and lead young people in a non-holistic expression of Christian spirituality that actually denies true happenings of their lives, thus silencing their cries? If so, this makes their form of Christianity anemic to the real, daily struggles that young people live. Consider the following cry.

"My God, my God . . . "

"My God, my God, why have you forsaken me?" These familiar, yet troubling words remind us of Jesus' last moments on the cross. How could God forsake and abandon Jesus in his hour of need? More will be shared about this question in chapter 2, but for now I simply note that Jesus relied on his Jewish spiritual tradition in his hour of need and pain. Jesus recited the first verse of Psalm 22, a psalm of lament. He was not at all abandoned by God, but rather God was with Jesus in his affliction.[10]

---

10. Johnson, "Jesus' Cry, God's Cry, and Ours," 80.

2. What kind of faith is being formed in adolescents?

The National Study of Youth and Religion (NSYR) published their findings in the book *Soul Searching: The Religious and Spiritual Lives of American Teenagers*. In regard to the type of faith being formed in young people, this study found that the spiritual and religious understanding among teens is very weak, and for the most part, they are inarticulate about their faith beliefs.[11] Religion operates in a weak social structural position compared to other activities and organizations that lay claim to their time, and so religion is simply not a big deal to youth. This study concluded that teenagers tend to espouse a religious outlook that is distinct and different from traditional faith commitments of most U.S. religious traditions, which can be described as Moralistic Therapeutic Deism (MTD)[12]:

1. A God exists who created and orders the world and watches over human life.

2. God wants people to be good, nice, and fair to each other, as taught in the Bible and by most world religions.

3. The central goal of life is to be happy and to feel good about oneself.

4. God does not need to be particularly involved in one's life except when God is needed to resolve a problem.

5. Good people go to heaven when they die.

If this outlook is common among young people, then we should be concerned with the image of God they possess. Their understanding is one that suggests God has a "hands off" approach in their daily affairs and is not too concerned about it, yet is some sort of "magic genie" who can be summoned at anytime to "fix" their problem in the way that they see fit. This image is a challenge for youthworkers as we seek to engage youth with the God of the Bible through Bible studies and other teachings, particularly when

11. Smith, *Soul Searching*, 260.

12. Ibid., 162–163.

teens consider themselves to be "the center", rather than God as Center and Creator. However, the NSYR suggests that this view from teens is primarily learned from their parents and other adults in their lives. In this respect, this is not solely a "youth problem," but a challenge for the broader church.

Another challenge that adult spiritual caregivers face today is the discretionary time and money our young people possess.[13] Media and marketing take advantage of this as products and experiences are shown to young people over and over, calling out for their time, money, and loyalty. However, there is a symbiotic relationship between youth and the media of youth culture. As music and media companies learn what sells to young people when new artists are introduced, they will spend millions of dollars in marketing to target and sell to the tastes of these young people. In this way, youth also possess an influential power on these companies.

In our individualistic, self-centered American society, "the culture assists individuals in making peace with whatever they choose as the path to personal fulfillment."[14] In this way our culture is therapeutic. Rather than confronting and challenging individual's beliefs, convictions, and commitments, popular culture simply gives the consumer what they want. And in this way, popular consumeristic culture shapes young people to ask, "How much more do I want?" rather than "Will this be good for my health and well-being? What impact will this have for others?"

Then, when our relatively old gadgets and toys do not satisfy our cravings, even though we may have purchased them a few months earlier, we will need something that is faster, louder, flashier, more extravagant, quicker to download, and more compact with bigger memory. Forces in our culture appeal to our sensate mentality that "is interested only in those things, usually the material in nature, that appeal to or affect our senses. It seeks the imposing, the impressive, the voluptuous; it encourages self-indulgence."[15] Before long, such a sensate worldview will have

13. Dunn, *Shaping the Spiritual Life of Students*, 37.

14. Ibid., 37.

15. Ibid., 39.

adolescents gauge the value of their lives by the level of sensory payoff.[16] We will have become pleasure pragmatists and possess an "If it feels good, do it" attitude. Again, this does not encourage us to consider how we or others are affected, except through sensory pleasure. These forces affect not only the faith of the youth being formed, but also our youth ministry efforts which may or may not mirror that of a consumeristic culture.

David White, in *Practicing Discernment with Youth: A Transformative Youth Ministry Approach*, argues that youth today are passive consumers compared to pre-Industrialized youth. The American educational system constantly seeks to prepare them for the future, rather than reflectively engage them in the present thus delaying their entrance into adulthood. The media market overwhelms young people by feeding off their youthful energies, yet this same market demands their compliance and passivity causing them to become detached from and numb to the material conditions around them.[17] Even our churches domesticate their prophetic voices and marginalize them from the larger faith community. This domestication distorts young people, rendering them apathetic, low in self-esteem, unstable in identity, and prone to violence or alienation.[18]

Furthermore, White contends that today's popular youth ministry efforts leave our young people ill equipped for lifelong discipleship.[19] In the past several decades, youth ministry had been left to independent commercial enterprises that failed to recognize one's own denomination, theology, ethnicity, and class, as well as lacked critique of social roles of young people. Discipleship, according to White, requires attentiveness to the holy, prophetic social critique, justice-seeking action, compassionate responses to all creation, and a commitment to transformative, mutual relationships that bring congruence to *imago dei* ("image of God").[20]

16. Ibid., 40.

17. White, *Practicing Discernment with Youth*, 17–19.

18. Ibid., 39.

19. Ibid., 5.

20. Ibid., vii.

What can we do as adult spiritual caregivers? How can we curb their focus on material success to include the real needs of the broken-hearted and impoverished around them? How can we better draw people into the larger faith community, both their immediate one and the historical one? How can we teach young people to engage in theological reflection and critique?

I suggest that engaging biblical lament can be one of those practices that will equip young people for lifelong discipleship. It will challenge them to reflect on their personal losses, as well as the suffering of other people around them and in the world. The practice of lament is a theological enterprise that demands they consider God's role in this world, as well as their own responsibilities. Doing so will engage them with their world and faith community, rather than passively sit on the sidelines. As adult spiritual caregivers lead young people in practices of biblical lament, we too will mature in our own faith while teaching youth necessary skills that brings the gospel into creative tension with the world around them. But what do I mean when I say "biblical lament"? I will offer a more detailed description and theological understanding in Chapter 2, but for now, consider the following overview.

What is biblical lament?

The biblical tradition of lament includes those prayers and expressions of complaint, anger, grief, despair, and protest to God.[21] Laments are to be understood as acts of persuasion so that God acts on behalf of the innocent, the victim, and the sufferer. It is not simply an act of mourning, but also an act of protest. The shape and structure of these prayers encourage the faith community to imitate it.[22] Lament is distinguished from mere complaint as it screams out the troubles and moves to some expression of confidence and assurance of being heard by God. Complaint offers only a sense of arguing with God about the present situation and

21. Billman and Migliore, *Rachel's Cry*, 6.
22. Brown and Miller, "Introduction," xiv–xv.

does not explicitly lead to trust in God. Since lament is a central element in biblical prayer, they should be part of our own prayers today, especially when nearly 40 percent of the Psalms are lament. This is the largest category of Psalms, by far outnumbering those of thanksgiving and praise.

A lingering question for me is if lament is so prevalent in the Psalms and a vital part of Old Testament Jewish spirituality, then why does it seem so foreign to our twenty-first century American world?

Overlooked by the Church?

Growing up in church I do not remember singing "cries against God" or "prayers of protest to Jesus." I was nurtured in a faith tradition that discouraged doubt in God. In fact, that would have been seen as a weakness in my faith. I was led to believe such feelings stemmed from some sort of sin in my life. Even though I had role models that allowed me to grieve some of my emotions, particularly in times of tragedy, I was not taught how that connected to my faith or understanding of God.

Biblical lament offers hope to adolescents in a way that connects them with God in an authentic, intimate manner. However, I believe the Christian church in the European-descended West has neglected practices of lament in worship, pastoral care, and biblical instruction. Overall, classical theologies of prayer have shown a deep ambivalence in what they say about the experience of grief and loss, and have not always known what to make of the lament prayer.[23] Church leaders have over-emphasized the penitential psalms, those which stem from personal or corporate sin. However, the penitential psalms "represent a distinct minority of the lament prayers in the Psalter. Far more frequent than penitential psalms are laments to God motivated by such experiences as

---

23. Billman and Migliore, *Rachel's Cry*, 46.

sickness, misfortune, unjust treatment by others, and personal or communal distress."[24]

Early Christian theology was dominated by Augustine. According to him, human beings are motivated by their desire for happiness, and "the Christian life is an arduous journey from destructive attachments to things of this world to the passionate love of God alone."[25] For the Christian, grief should be severely restrained, and so for Augustinian piety, "lament over loss of loved ones and delights of this world is replaced by confession of sins."[26] When it came to the Psalms, two features stood out for Augustine. First, he read them with a heavy Christological lens. For example, the cry of abandonment in Psalm 22 was interpreted as words of a dying Savior, not to be uttered by other humans as their own expression to God. Second, he construed the lament psalms as penitential psalms, and so once again emphasizing the sinful state of humanity. "While Augustine acknowledges the appropriateness of lament in the mode of grieving for our sins, he is at least uncomfortable and even suspicious of lament for the loss of a beloved family member or intimate friend or in response to a calamity such as the exile and enslavement of a whole people. In the Augustinian piety of detachment, grief over such losses would be misdirected."[27]

Reformation theologian Martin Luther's piety and theology focused on his doctrine of justification by grace through faith alone. Prayer is rooted in the fact that God wants us to do this and so we are also not only to offer prayer with our words, but also with our whole heart. The Psalms were important for him, but they were only second to the Lord's Prayer in instructing Christians how and what to pray.[28] When it comes to lament, though, Christians are to pray the laments, while the grace of God is the only consolation in our experiences of loneliness, despair, and

24. Ibid., 29.
25. Ibid., 47.
26. Ibid., 48.
27. Ibid., 50.
28. Ibid., 51.

abandonment. Compared to Augustine, Luther shows a remarkable freedom in allowing the expression of lament, but he is careful not to grant attacks on God's gracious promises as the psalmist suggests in some of the prayers. Furthermore, he continues to view the lament psalms as that of penitential, though not to the degree of Augustine because he "thinks exclusively of the sinner's utter dependence on the sheer and miraculous forgiveness of God."[29]

Calvin, another sixteenth century Reformer, viewed Augustine as the greatest of early church theologians. Though he also believed that the grief of the Christian ought to be tempered, it was not due to us being worldly sinful beings. Instead it is because we are called to submit to the providence of God in all events.[30] Calvin believed that prayer was the chief exercise of faith, and that in this act Christians were to bring all their needs, anxieties, praise, and thanksgiving to God. Though Psalms is the primary book of prayer for Christians and prayers of lament are allowed, they must be kept within the context of submission to God's will and God's providential care. Therefore, he calls Christians to humility and patience in the face of adversity. "For Calvin, we should always be ready to confess our sins and manifest patience in suffering, showing moderation in expressions of sorrow because to do otherwise would be to doubt the fatherly governance of God. When adversity strikes us, God is either punishing us for our sins or purifying us for closer communion with God."[31]

Even my own Anabaptist/Mennonite faith tradition has overlooked the act of biblical lament. Early Anabaptism was not so much influenced by one particular leader of faith, but by various people and collective experiences. Suffering and persecution was at the core of early Anabaptist beginnings that evolved during early Protestant Reformation efforts in various pockets throughout Europe. Two early books detail the stories, songs, and prayers of early Anabaptist faith martyrs as a way to encourage the believers and to pass on faith to the next generations.

29. Ibid., 55.
30. Ibid., 56–57.
31. Ibid., 60.

The *Ausbund*, first printed in 1564, was one of the first song collections to ever be published. It is still used today among Old Order Amish in North America.[32] Singing was a part of daily life in the sixteenth century and served as a carrier and communicator of early Anabaptist teaching. This hymnbook encapsulated central Anabaptist beliefs, kept alive the stories of martyrs, and taught liturgical doctrines and prayer, such as the Apostles Creed and the Lord's Prayer. These songs were not explicitly examples of lament, but were faith exhortations stemming out of a painful reality.

Martyrs Mirror, first published in 1660 by Dutch Mennonite minister Thieleman van Braght, is a collection of stories of early Christian and Anabaptist martyrs. van Braght spent years researching these Christians who died for their faith. He hoped this would encourage his church members in their faith because "[h]e worried that too many Mennonites in his day were becoming wealthy and lax in their Christian commitments."[33] Then, in 1748 faced with the possibility of war, Mennonites living in Pennsylvania had *Martyrs Mirror* translated from Dutch into German, their first language, to serve as a witness of history and remind them of Christ's way of love. "They hoped that the stories of discipleship and nonresistance recorded in its pages would encourage the church to remain faithful to the gospel of peace."[34]

Over the years Mennonites have often carried a humble, passive acceptance of suffering and discipleship stemming from their earliest roots. "Again and again it is affirmed that suffering is the true sign of being a Christian and of being a member of the true church. Suffering for Christ's sake is identified as the nearest, most direct way of gaining eternal life."[35] The early Anabaptist acceptance of suffering by the hands of other faith traditions may have been an appropriate response in the sixteenth century, but it also fostered in Mennonites a sense of passive acceptance of wrongdoing done against them. The songs and prayers of praise and

---

32. Snyder, *Anabaptist History and Theology*, 107.

33. Loewen and Nolt, *Through Fire and Water*, 170.

34. Ibid., 169.

35. Klaassen, *Anabaptism in Outline*, 85.

adoration to God in the midst of persecution does not follow the biblical pattern of lament. In fact, arguing with and blaming God for such atrocities was not something performed by Anabaptists. Therefore, even though this expression of acceptance of the cost of discipleship is something to be admired, it also denies truth-telling and speaking out in protest of wrongful deeds.

These theological streams have greatly impacted the Western Christian Church, including the engagement of biblical lament. Though there is significant emphasis on the role of sin in the lives of humans, there is not an appreciation for connecting with God through expressions of biblical lament. Either it is simply inappropriate to call out to God in such anger, or the reason for our grief is due to our sin. Therefore, lament has lost favor with the Christian church in the West. This may be an oversimplification of the church's treatment of biblical lament, but the point is that there has been a neglect of proper, biblical engagement of this form of spirituality.

Adults who neglect to teach adolescents and model for them the ways of biblical lament, only perpetuate the next generation's ignorance of this vital form of connection to God. In a country that is witnessing an increase in adolescent suffering, I believe biblical lament is Good News for adolescents and adults alike. Similarly, long-time youth ministry professor Dean Borgman simply states, "The church has not given youth a chance to lament or confess appropriately, even though youth feel a need, subconsciously perhaps, for public and private expression of despair and remorse."[36]

For the Sake of the Gospel . . .

For the sake of the Gospel and its relevance to our world today, biblical lament needs to be a fundamental aspect of our Christian faith. Leaders must assist people in engaging this expression of faith in both personal devotions and in corporate worship settings. Old Testament theologian Patrick Miller suggests that to take steps

36. Borgman, *Hear My Story*, 380.

in recovering aspects of lament for our faith, we need to heed three voices of lament: the human voice, the voice of Christ, and the voice of the world.[37]

The voice of the human cries to God for help in the midst of injustice and suffering. This is consistent throughout the whole of scripture. Lament is not only the voice of pain, but also that of prayer. The voice of Christ recalls the utterances of Jesus on the cross reminding us that suffering is not the last word and that he died for our suffering as much as for our sins.[38] The voice of the world calls us as Christ's followers to give attention to it in the same way that Christ listened. Laments are prayers for help and for justice.[39] Today, I believe young people are crying out through their cutting, anxiety-induced illnesses, and other expressions of self-harm.

Everyday Losses and Shipwrecks

Yes, there are those times when the church may turn to biblical lament after some serious tragedy, death, or destruction, but what about the "little losses" that accompany life on a daily basis? For adolescents, they encounter many changes physically, developmentally, socially, emotionally, mentally, and spiritually. There must be ways that we as their spiritual caregivers can aid and accompany them that lead to healthier expressions of life than through suicide attempts and increased mental health illnesses. Take my wife for example. As a young child her parents divorced; this was her mother's second marriage. Then as an early adolescent her mother's third marriage failed. These and other losses that she experienced throughout her teenage years were not properly dealt with in constructive ways. Soon after graduating from high school and entering the military she developed an eating disorder. She struggled with this for several years as a late adolescent even though she sought help and treatment, but parts of her story

---

37. Miller, "Heaven's Prisoners," 15.

38. Ibid., 21.

39. Ibid., 23–24.

suggest that this eating disorder was a result of unattended losses during her early and middle adolescent years.

Humans of all ages encounter change and loss on a regular basis in ways that go unattended and unacknowledged, but also consider the following image from Sharon Daloz Parks. She suggests that many adolescents will encounter another type of significant loss at some point in their lives, a "metaphorical shipwreck," in which she states:[40]

> Metaphorical shipwreck may occur with the loss of a relationship, violence to one's property, collapse of a career venture, physical illness or injury, defeat of a cause, a fateful choice that irrevocably reorders one's life, betrayal by a community or government, or the discovery that an intellectual construct is inadequate. Sometimes we simply encounter someone or some new experience or idea that calls into question things as we have perceived them or as they were taught to us or as we had read, heard, or assumed. This kind of experience can suddenly rip into the fabric of life, or it may slowly yet just as surely unravel the meanings that have served as the home of the soul.

Though her writing is primarily concerned with late adolescents, the reality is that most early and middle adolescents are heading for such a shipwreck experience before successfully navigating their way into adulthood. The years leading up to that significant change and loss is critical for how they are prepared to deal with it.

For Daloz Parks, this metaphor of shipwreck describes that jolt that many young adults may experience as they seek to make sense of their past while discovering who they will be in the future. The shelter and protection of the past that once carried them through no longer does. However, on the other side of this shipwreck is a gladness that "arises from an embracing, complex kind of knowing that is experienced as a more trustworthy understanding of reality in both its beauty and terror . . . The power of the experience of shipwreck is located precisely in one's inability to immediately sense the promise of anything beyond the breakup of what has been secure

40. Daloz Parks, *Big Questions, Worthy Dreams*, 39.

and trustworthy . . . Then, when we are met by the surprise of new meaning, we are amazed. Passover is the celebration of amazement. Easter is what happens to us when we look back and say, 'I survived that?!' Faith is informed by joy as well as by pain."[41] But for this expression of hope to be realized in the midst of this disorienting experience, there needs to be a certain level of maturity of faith and understanding of meaning-making which may be difficult to find in most young people. This is one reason why young people need mature adult spiritual caregivers to be with them and guide them through these pivotal, life-shaping moments.

I employ Daloz Parks's concept of the metaphorical shipwreck, not to suggest that adolescence is one big, long shipwreck—I do not believe this to be the case at all!—but to remind ourselves that part of the journey of adolescence is that of discovery of identity, meaning, and purpose. At some point, for faith to mature, young people will need to question what they have been taught and articulate it in ways that makes sense to them. However, this can be a very disorienting experience. Therefore, the role of adult spiritual caregivers who can walk with young people and help them discern what is happening to them is crucial for their hope and maturation. But accompanying that time of questioning and meaning-making is that of loss—a loss of what was familiar, comfortable, and at times easy.

In addition to the losses arising from the more normal and expected developmental changes are those that thrust young people into a shipwreck experience before they are emotionally mature: the death of a parent, a serious injury or illness, the divorce of their parents, or a geographic move. When these various losses occur, how will they make sense of it all? What will the language be for them to describe their experience? Will they connect it with their faith and with the broader story of God and God's people? Or will it be divorced from such an understanding, and therefore make faith irrelevant and impotent? How will we as adult spiritual caregivers journey with adolescents in their many experiences of life?

41. Ibid., 43.

A Way of Being in Ministry To/With Adolescents . . .

I propose that engaging practices of biblical lament will help young people live through not only the major losses of life, but also those which occur from an everyday basis. Engaging lament will help give language to their lived-out experiences of life and consider how this might fit within the broader God-story, thus informing their developing faith.

I believe lament is a missing, crucial ingredient for how we minister to and with young people. This engagement with biblical lament is not meant to serve as a new model for youth ministry, but a way of being in the midst of adolescent ministry. Lament brings the particularity of one's suffering to voice,[42] it offers a form or structure for expressing such suffering,[43] and it enables the community a way of opportunity for healing to occur.[44] Overall, engaging practices of biblical lament and the accompanying hope it can provide is a gift of empowerment. The experience of any kind of suffering, no matter the degree, makes people vulnerable. "Suffering involves feelings of powerlessness because the event that has occasioned the suffering is beyond the sufferer's control and the feelings evoked by the event are often experienced as out of the sufferer's control as well."[45] For many adolescents, certain levels of suffering, isolation, confusion, doubt, and pain are an everyday experience.

Conclusion

As we seek to help young people and ourselves faithfully respond to Christ's call in this world, praying our own laments and attuning ourselves to the work of Christ will sharpen our ears to the suffering within us and around us. Recovering lament in our faith will guide us through not only our own abandonment issues and

42. Billman and Migliore, *Rachel's Cry*, 80.

43. Ibid., 83.

44. Ibid., 86.

45. Ibid., 94.

times of forsakenness, but also foster a more sympathetic and understanding posture to friends, family, and others facing similar situations of vulnerability and pain. But this compassionate stance is merely the first step in more active expressions of intercession and responses to the needs. For too long our American society has emphasized success and decried suffering and loss as signs of failure. It is time that we Christians strive for faithfulness rather than "success" that denies, hides, and oppresses. Engaging practices of biblical lament matures our faithfulness to Christ's call and the Gospel.

The remainder of this book will elaborate on the need for engagement of practices of biblical lament, suggest practical ways this can be done, and explore the relevance of biblical lament in ministry to/with adolescents through the perspectives of the voice of Christ/God, the human voice, and the voice of the world. Chapter 2 will offer us a glimpse of God's view of this type of spiritual expression, primarily through the work of Psalms and Lamentations, and offer some suggestions of how we may embody aspects of that spirituality with our young people today. Chapters 3 through 5 will help us to understand the voice of the human adolescent and that of the broader adolescent world by hearing about a research project I conducted with several youth groups, by examining more closely the progression of the adolescent voice through beginning, middle, and end of adolescence, and by considering some contemporary sociological and lived-out realities of our times. Though these chapters are an intermingling swirl of both the human voice and the voice of the world, the role of biblical lament will be incorporated in this section and continue to serve as the voice of Christ/God. Chapter 6 will offer additional practical suggestions for ways to engage biblical lament.

2

Theology of Biblical Lament

Introduction to Biblical Lament

"My God, my God . . . "

"My God, my God, why have you forsaken me?" These familiar, yet troubling words remind us of Jesus' last moments on the cross. How could God forsake and abandon Jesus in his hour of need? We might answer this troubling question one of two ways. One, this crucifixion event was so painful for God that God simply needed to look away because never before had such an act occurred. Or two, it was okay for Jesus to talk to God this way because Jesus was God. Both of these options view the uttered cry by Jesus as a true historical event, and so God must have forsaken Jesus or Jesus was a liar.

However, in this passage Jesus relies on his Jewish spiritual tradition. In his hour of need and pain, Jesus recalls the first verse of Psalm 22, a psalm of lament. Jesus was not abandoned by God, but God was with Jesus in his affliction.[1] A short time later when Jesus gave up his last breath, the curtain in the Holy Temple was torn in two from top to bottom (Mark 15:38; Matthew 27:51). As a response to Jesus' own naked cry from the cross, God unveiled Godself in a way that left God vulnerably exposed to humanity.[2] Robert Dykstra, pastoral theologian, suggests, "In Jesus' cry, God

1. Johnson, "Jesus' Cry, God's Cry, and Ours," 80.
2. Dykstra, "Rending the Curtain," 60.

cries too; and in Jesus' cry, our own cries are validated by God and will be redeemed. In short, God is at work in Jesus' cry to hear us, to save us, and to empower us, so that in response to this God who refuses to let us go, we too, by the Spirit's power, can resolve not to abandon one another."[3]

To better understand the cry of Jesus and God's response to this cry, let us further understand what biblical lament is and its role within Jewish spirituality. In this chapter I will overview biblical lament and its function, with primary attention to the Psalms and Lamentations, and offer suggestions for how lament might be embodied today.

What is biblical lament?

The biblical tradition of lament includes those prayers and expressions of complaint, anger, grief, despair, and protest to God.[4] Old Testament scholar Kathleen O'Conner suggests they are prayers that "erupt from wounds, burst out of unbearable pain, and bring it to language . . . They take anger and despair before God and community. They grieve. They argue. They find fault . . . Although laments appear disruptive of God's world, they are acts of fidelity. In vulnerability and honesty, they cling to God and demand for God to see, hear, and act . . . in the process of harsh complaint and resistance, they also express faith in God in the midst of chaos, doubt, and confusion."[5]

The shape and structure of these prayers impress itself upon the community of faith that merits imitation.[6] The structure itself may be a vehicle for one presently praying to move beyond their predicament to a new level of trust and confidence. Lament is distinguished from mere complaint. The former bemoans the troubles and moves to some expression of confidence and assurance

---

3. Johnson, "Jesus' Cry, God's Cry, and Ours," 80–81.

4. Billman and Migliore, *Rachel's Cry*, 6.

5. O'Conner, *Lamentations and the Tears of the World*, 9.

6. Brown and Miller, "Introduction," xiv–xv.

of being heard, whereas the latter offers only a sense of arguing with God about the present situation and does not explicitly lead to trust in God. Nevertheless, complaint is part of biblical prayer as well as a function within lament, and is itself an act of trust. At the center of these prayers are petitions for God's help. Since lament and complaint are central elements in biblical prayer, they should be part of our own prayers today. Overall, these prayers are to be understood as acts of persuasion so that God acts on behalf of the innocent, the victim, and the sufferer.

Regarding the structure of the lament itself, Old Testament scholar Walter Brueggemann suggests there are six regular elements to Israel's classic model.[7] First, God is addressed and named, thereby trusting that God is listening attentively. Second, the lament moves to a complaint that identifies the trouble. Third, flow moves to petition where the author demands that God acts, moves, and saves. Fourth, motivations are added to the petition which give God additional reasons for acting. Fifth, due to the extreme pain, the lamenter does not stop at petition for rescue but may often ask for vengeance or ill to befall the enemy. Finally, after uttering the need, the hurt, the demand, and the venom something unexpected happens. The mood and the tone change to praise, confidence, and gratitude of God. It is not completely known why this turn happens, but the speaker is at a very different place than when the prayer began. However, not all six of these elements are used in every lament or occur in the same sequential order.

These six elements of lament can be categorized into two basic parts: the plea and the praise.[8] The plea is the complaint that somehow God should correct the skewed situation. It includes the address to God, the complaint, the petition, the motivations, and the imprecation or voice of vengeance. The praise signifies a change and recognizes that things are now different. Features of praise include the assurance of being heard, payment of vows, and doxology. Brueggemann states:

---

7. Weems, *Psalms of Lament*, x–xi.

8. Brueggemann, *The Message of the Psalms*, 54–56.

> We cannot ever know whether it is changed circum-
> stance, or changed attitude, or something of both. But
> the speaker now speaks differently. Now the sense of
> urgency and desperation is replaced with joy, gratitude,
> and well-being . . . Thus the sequence of *complaint-praise*
> is a necessary and legitimate way with God, each part
> in its own, appropriate time. But one moment is not
> less faithful than the other . . . It is the honest address to
> God that moves the relationship to new possibilities of
> faithfulness that can only be reached through such risky
> honesty. In the full relationship, the *season of plea* must
> be taken as seriously as the *season of praise.*[9]

It is important to note that we do not know how long it took
the authors to write their laments. And though there seems to be
a structured form and flow to biblical lament, we dare not think
that in our desperate hour of need we can simply pray through
this formula and be at a different place a few minutes after beginning our prayer. Perhaps it took the original composers days,
weeks, months, or even years to get to a point of appropriately
praising God. Therefore, we should be careful not to place guilt
upon ourselves or others if we are not in a genuine state of praise
and thanksgiving to God. In other words, even though there is a
pivotal and transformative turn, we do not know the amount of
time that lapsed before the author reached that point.

Another significant feature of lament is that it is not simply
an act of mourning; it is an act of protest. Brueggemann states,
"The lament-complaint, perhaps Israel's most characteristic and
vigorous mode of faith, introduces us to a 'spirituality of protest.'
That is, Israel boldly recognizes that all is not right in the world.
This is against our easy gentile way of denial, pretending in each
other's presence and in the presence of God that 'all is well,'
when it is not."[10]

To truly understand that lament is an act of protest, we
need to know that it is distinguishable from two other types of
prayers found in the Bible: penitential prayers and funeral dirges.

9. Ibid., 56–57.
10. Weems, *Psalms of Lament*, xii.

Penitential prayers, or prayers of confession, express a strong sense of guilt and remorse for personal or corporate sins. They plea to God for forgiveness and renewal, but "the primary emphasis of the prayer of lament is not on the grievous sins of those who pray but on their misery, their sense of suffering unjustly, and their feeling of being abandoned by friends and even by God."[11] Funeral dirges are acts of mourning connected to the burial of the dead. They forewarn against or commemorate the fact of a death and/ or destruction. Though both genres of lament and funeral dirge are about loss and suffering, the former is "a plea for help in the terrible moment of suffering and loss, while the dirge, also an act of lamenting, mourns the loss."[12]

Biblical Overview of Lament and Its Function

Though biblical laments may be most associated with those found in the Psalms, they do appear elsewhere in the Bible throughout the Old and New Testaments. However, over time their purpose and role within the life of the faith community changed. Today, there are some, including myself, in the United States who feel that lament has been almost nonexistent in the United States and so a sort of reclaiming or renewal is needed. Old Testament scholar Claus Westermann infers that "Jewish spirituality, with its vigorous prayers of protest, differs sharply from much Christian spirituality that often extols the virtues of submissiveness and passive acceptance of suffering."[13] How did we get from an ancient Jewish people who regularly engaged in lament to a Christian tradition in the United States who, though claiming to have folded this ancient tradition into its own history, neglects lament?

To begin, one must recognize the lament genre itself evolved during the Old Testament times: early (pre-kingdom), middle (kingdom), and late (post-kingdom). Westermann suggests that

11. Billman and Migliore, *Rachel's Cry*, 7.

12. Brown and Miller, "Introduction," xvi.

13. Billman and Migliore, *Rachel's Cry*, 25.

biblical lament commonly contained three components or dimensions corresponding to its three subjects: God, the one who laments, and the enemy.[14] He states:

> In the early period, the dominant one of the three components constituting the lament is the lament directed at God, the complaint against God. In the middle period, that is, in the Psalms, the three components of the lament are on the whole held in balance. In the later period, the complaint against God falls almost totally silent. How and why it becomes silent can easily be observed.
>
> The theology of the Deuteronomic school—which declared the history of the wilderness sojourn and even more the history of established Israel, to be a history of disobedience, and which sought to prove that political annihilation was the righteous judgment of God—began to formulate a way of thinking in which complaint against God was absolutely disallowed. The guilt of the Patriarchs was so earnestly and consciously taken over that, in place of the complaint against God formerly found in laments concerned with the fate of the nation, now the exact opposite appeared, viz., the justification of God's righteousness or simply praise of the righteous God. Nevertheless, over and beyond this theological conviction, perplexity at the incomprehensible judgments of God remained.[15]

In the early period, Westermann identifies themes of affliction of the people, including questions related to the meaning of existence, such as "Why?" and "If this be so, why do I live?" The lament was offered by a mediator, such as a judge or prophet like in Judges 15:18 (a lament of Samson), Genesis 25:22 and Genesis 27:46 (prayers of Rebekah), and the laments of Moses. The middle period includes the writings of the Psalms. The later period includes four different types of laments found in the Apocrypha and Pseudepigrapha, including those similar to ones found in the Psalter, petitionary prayers without a lament, prayers of repentance,

14. Westermann, *Praise and Lament in the Psalms*, 169.

15. Ibid., 171–172.

and free-standing laments that emerge from and alongside prayer but mainly as complaint. Of these four, the second category is most prevalent demonstrating that the lament has been reduced to petition.[16]

To summarize the pre-New Testament Jewish era, Westermann suggests that the lament is an event among the one who laments, God, and "the enemy" which arose from a situation of great need. The practice of calling on God in times of need existed in Israel from the earliest to the latest periods of her history, "but the way in which one called upon God changed dramatically. In the early period the bare lament, without following petition, constituted this call. In the Psalms the lament is consistently followed by a petition, i.e., a supplication for help. In the late period the petition is separated from the lament, and an associated phenomenon is the gradual disintegration of the Psalm of lament as a whole."[17]

In the Christian New Testament era, the writers urged the faith community to constantly be involved in prayer, but unlike the Old Testament Psalms, these authors do not provide us with many actual prayers. However, it is important to remember that the Old Testament was the holy book for early Christian communities.[18] Kathleen Billman and Daniel Migliore pick up the question left by Westermann: Does the loss of lament in the prayer and worship of the Christian church today have its basis in the New Testament itself? Their thesis contends "that while not as prominent as in the Old Testament, strands of prayer of lament and protest are not only present in the New Testament but are found at decisive points in the story that it tells."[19]

They suggest these prayers, including the Lord's prayer, are full of passion and a sense of urgency. Like the Old Testament, these prayers have a particular life context and "are prayers of a beleaguered and persecuted minority."[20] Prayer includes petition

16. Ibid., 201.

17. Ibid., 213.

18. Billman and Migliore, *Rachel's Cry,* 33.

19. Ibid., 34.

20. Ibid., 35.

for the forgiveness of sins, but is not reduced solely to that because Jesus' ministry was wider than solely the forgiveness of sins. They suggest, "it is inappropriate to reduce the lament that arises from suffering to the plea for forgiveness . . . the salvation and healing which Jesus brings in his ministry and in his death and resurrection are a deliverance from inexplicable suffering as well as from human sin."[21] Though prayers of vengeance are not as numerable in the New Testament, "its presence reminds us of the seriousness of evil and the reality of divine judgment. In the book of Revelation we find prayers that resemble the plea for vengeance on enemies present in some of the Old Testament psalms of lament."[22]

There are other prayers of struggle, like those called out by Jesus in Gethsemane and Paul for the removal of his "thorn in the flesh."[23] Other passages breathe the spirit of lament and protest, such as in Mark 4:38 ("Teacher, do you not care that we are perishing?"), Luke 18:1-8 (The parable of the widow and unjust judge; she remained persistent in her demand for justice.),[24] and Jesus' use of Psalm 22 in his awful cry of abandonment on the cross in Mark 15:34 ("My God, my God, why have you forsaken me?") which directly connect with the spiritual tradition of lament. "Because the New Testament community sees Jesus in the most intimate relationship to God, the lament of Jesus becomes the basis of Christian affirmation that God also laments."[25] In spite of the various connections to the New Testament, Billman and Migliore contend:

> Despite the evidences of the persistence of the lament prayer in the New Testament . . . , there can be no denying that some passages of the New Testament show a tendency to mute the lament tradition . . . It is also apparent in some passages . . . where Christians are counseled not to lament but to show patience and endurance in the face of suffering (James 5:7-18). Still we would argue that, at

21. Ibid., 36.
22. Ibid., 36.
23. Ibid., 36.
24. Ibid., 37–38.
25. Ibid., 39.

its center, the New Testament like the Old acknowledges the reality of evil and suffering and gives voice to the mourning of the afflicted and the longing for justice and renewal of life. Furthermore, like the Old Testament, the gospel tradition refuses to equate suffering with sin. In addition, the New Testament like the Old includes lament in tensive juxtaposition with the praise of God rather than as an end in itself. Finally, the faith of both Old and New Testament envisions a God who without ceasing to be God shares the lamentation of a groaning creation.[26]

To better grasp the role and function of biblical lament, I will now further explore two books of the Bible, Psalms and Lamentations, and how to embody each today.

Psalms of Lament

Psalms is the ancient prayer book which shaped Jewish spirituality. Since these writings were incorporated into the Christian tradition, we can assume its formational influence impacted the followers of Jesus as well. Though there are many wonderful psalms of praise and thanksgiving to God, there are also those of negativity, complaint, cries for vengeance and penitence that are foundational to a life of faith with God. Brueggemann contends, "Much Christian piety and spirituality is romantic and unreal in its positiveness. As children of Enlightenment, we have censored and selected around the voice of darkness and disorientation, seeking to go from strength to strength, victory to victory. But such a way not only ignores the Psalms; it is a lie in terms of our experience . . . The Psalms are profoundly subversive of the dominant culture, which wants to deny and cover over the darkness we are called to enter."[27]

The Psalms dialogically express both sides of the faith conversation between God and humanity. Even though there are one hundred fifty Psalms, it seems the Christian tradition has a tendency to reduce the ones actually read in public, recited, and

26. Ibid., 40.

27. Brueggemann, *Spirituality of the Psalms*, xii.

studied to a handful of well-loved Psalms like Psalm 23 (The Good Shepherd) and Psalm 139 (God knowing our innermost being). How then do we work towards maintaining a balance in Psalmic spirituality? How do we make sense of such a vast collection of prayers and songs that span a period over two thousand years ago?

Before taking a closer look at the psalms of lament and work towards discovering answers to those challenges, I draw upon the scholarly work of Walter Brueggemann as he identifies three general Psalmic types: psalms of orientation, psalms of disorientation, and psalms of new orientation. "It is suggested that the psalms can be roughly grouped this way, and the flow of human life characteristically is located either in the actual experience of one of these settings or is in movement from one to another."[28]

Psalms of Orientation include those hymns of creation, Torah, wisdom, retribution, and well-being. These Psalms "were created, transmitted, valued, and relied upon by a community of faithful people. To these people, their faith was both important and satisfying."[29] The Psalms of Disorientation include the laments. They recognize that "life is also savagely marked by incoherence, a loss of balance, and unrelieved symmetry."[30] Finally, the Psalms of New Orientation include those of thanksgiving and certain aspects of praise that stem out of a disoriented experience. Of these categories of Psalms, the largest number is those of Disorientation.

There are two basic types of Disorientation lament psalms: individual and communal. The individual laments, which comprise a large number of these psalms, signify that something is amiss in the relationship and that it must be righted. These are the voices of those who find their circumstances quite dangerous. In fact, Brueggemann indicates, "These are the speeches of caged men and women getting familiar with their new place . . . It is the function of these songs to enable, require, and legitimate the complete rejection of the old orientation."[31] The lament of the indi-

28. Ibid., 8.
29. Ibid., 16.
30. Ibid., 25.
31. Ibid., 39.

vidual is the single most extensive form found within the Psalms. Its theological significance lies in the fact that it gives voice to the suffering. "The lament is the language of suffering; in it suffering is given the dignity of language. It will not stay silent!"[32]

It is not consistently clear the cause of the individual's suffering, though the lament is often over physical or spiritual distress. Sometimes God is accused as the cause, and other times it is the "enemy" who threatens the lamenter and directs their hostility on to the lamenting individual. "The lamenter alone is under duress. Never is it even implied that the lamenter belongs to a circle of friends who are being assailed . . . Moreover, the enemy so absolutely overwhelms the lamenter, so completely undoes him, that the idea of opposing the enemy never comes to mind."[33] Furthermore, "the relationship of the lamenter to those who he accuses is one which remains within the community to which both belong . . . The foundation of the community is its relationship to God."[34]

The communal and national laments, which are fewer in number, are statements about the religious dimension of public events of loss. "They permit us to remember that we are indeed public citizens and creatures and have an immediate, direct, and personal stake in public events."[35] The complaint against God is a dominant feature with these types of psalms. "The heart of the lament of the people in ancient Israel lies in these accusatory questions and statements directed at God." [36] In fact, there are no communal laments void of this. Another characteristic is their complaint about an enemy. Unlike those of individual laments, it is clear that the enemy is a recognizable political adversary who has dealt a severe blow to them and caused their suffering.[37] "The

---

32. Westermann, *Praise and Lament in the Psalms,* 272.

33. Ibid., 193.

34. Ibid., 193–194.

35. Brueggemann, *Spirituality of the Psalms,* 40.

36. Westermann, *Praise and Lament in the Psalms,*177–178.

37. Ibid., 193.

theological significance of the national lament lies in its immediate relationship to the activity of God as Savior."[38]

Though the communal laments are not as numerous as the individual ones, they are important for the nurture of responsible faith. "The recovery of the personal complaint psalms is a great gain, but unless the communal complaints are set alongside them, the record of personal religion can serve only privatistic concerns—and that is no doubt a betrayal of biblical faith."[39]

Embodying the Psalms of Lament Today

In most cases we do not know the specific reasons for what prompted the psalms of lament. However, these psalms "invite personal and communal identification with the emotional, relational, and spiritual worlds of the psalmist as the psalmist oscillates between feelings and faith."[40] Therefore, the identification with the psalmist may in fact become a source of transformation and healing for people today. In the remainder of this section on the Psalms of Lament, I wish to offer some thoughts as to why and how we may embody its message of good news today.

In her article "Recovering Lamentation as a Practice in the Church," Nancy Duff argues "that the practice of lament needs to be recovered in the church and that psalms of lament can be used to encourage the Christian church today to allow room for true lamentation in our corporate and individual lives of prayer and worship."[41] She addresses three aspects of these psalms that can aid us today. "Psalms of lament (1) challenge our inability to acknowledge the intense emotions that grief entails, (2) free us to make a bold expression of grief before God and in the presence of others,

---

38. Ibid., 270.
39. Brueggemann, *Spirituality of the Psalms*, 41–42.
40. Hamman, *When Steeples Cry*, 123.
41. Duff, "Recovering Lamentation as a Practice in the Church," 4.

and (3) allow us to rely on God and the community to carry forth hope on our behalf when we ourselves have no hope in us."[42]

First, Duff contends that our society and church discourage us from expressing intense feelings of sorrow or anger when we experience significant loss.[43] We may be encouraged to simply "get over it" and move on in life. To come to terms with our inability to face grief honestly, we must acknowledge that the Bible recognizes the overwhelming reality of grief that cannot be consoled and that "the church needs to turn to the biblical concept of lament to provide a space where people can express their sorrow before God and one another."[44]

She then suggests that simply reading and understanding the lament psalms provide an avenue to create space and freedom to express the powerful emotions that often accompany grief. This also informs the reader that they are not the first to feel abandoned by God.[45] Furthermore, even if the reader does not personally identify with the words of a particular psalm, they can read it as a prayer on behalf of another whose experience is that of the psalmist.[46] In this way it serves as a type of intercessory prayer.

Finally, Duff acknowledges that there are situations in life where God might be the only one to offer words of hope. To illustrate this point, she recalls the "slaughter of the innocents" in Matthew 2. Rachel refuses to be consoled, but yet the Gospel honors her refusal as "faithful testimony."[47] In reality, this implies that in those worst instances of grief and despair, our own offerings of hope to the grieved must be spoken carefully and respectfully.

Michael Jinkins asks the question in his book *In the House of the Lord: Inhabiting the World of the Psalms*: What would it mean for us to learn to inhabit the world of the psalms? He poses three answers to this question. First, it "allows us to enter into a world

42. Ibid., 4.

43. Ibid., 5.

44. Ibid., 7.

45. Ibid., 10.

46. Ibid., 8.

47. Ibid., 11.

where we recognize the reign of the Lord."[48] These psalms offer a language that acknowledges God as Sovereign, not Self, and thereby inhabiting a language helps us inhabit the world. However, we must also recognize that taking seriously such a world requires that we be bilingual and possess "the ability to move around in the language modes and thought patterns of the Bible and our own cultures."[49] Second, we need "to practice the habituation of God as a living discipline."[50] Habitual practice through reading and praying these psalms will form our character, and so it is essential that we remain committed to them even when life is not so joyful. Third, inhabiting this world guides us to "discern the sacred quality of all life, the whole of creation."[51] Jinkins contends that the Psalms "stubbornly refuse to respect the dichotomy we commonly recognize between the sacred and the secular, the holy and the profane . . . Creation shares God's holiness, because the Holy One forms creation and breathes life into it."[52] However, he also recognizes that this glory-filled creation is not synonymous with God. Nevertheless, Jinkins suggests that the paradox in the world of the psalmist is that the closer we get to God, the more clearly we see that we are mere creatures and only God is God. "By discerning and respecting this infinite qualitative difference between God the holy Creator and this creaturely world that belongs to God, we prepare ourselves to see the awesomeness and mystery of both God and creation."[53]

As Jinkins considers the role of the faith community in inhabiting these psalms, he asks the following questions: "What can we say, then about the relationship between these communities of faith and the psalms of lament? What might it mean for us in our communities of faith to enter into the world of the psalms? First, we must recognize that the communities 'lost in the midst'

48. Jinkins, *In the House of the Lord*, 3.

49. Ibid., 5.

50. Ibid., 18.

51. Ibid., 23.

52. Ibid., 23.

53. Ibid., 28.

of the psalms of lament wrote, and we hear these words, out of the depths of their own profoundly lamentable history."[54] They knew first-hand suffering, grief, despair, famine, persecution, warfare, betrayal, and false accusations. Second, in spite of their painful historical realities, they "believed that God could be trusted, could be called upon and counted on in all of life. Whatever the form of distress took, they placed themselves in God's hands."[55]

Finally, Jinkins suggest that we locate ourselves in the psalms of lament. To do so acknowledges we understand "the psalms remain tenaciously performative. Thus, when we approach the psalms of lament, we are attracted to them not for the information they impart nor even their evocative power. They invite, or, perhaps better, they compel us to participate with them in lamentation. The hearer of the psalm of lament is transformed into the speaker."[56] In other words as we perform these psalms both in our liturgical and pastoral uses, let us remember the formational and shaping influence they have on us as individuals and as a faith community. Therefore, it is essential that we not shy away from speaking these psalms in worship, youth group meetings, Bible study, pastoral care, and private devotions, even if the words may seem unpleasant at times. Inhabiting these words and worlds of the psalmists will enable us to better grasp the significance of these psalms and open us to the transformative power of God as articulated in these prayers of deep faith.

Lamentations

Having described biblical lament within the Psalms, I now turn our attention to Lamentations. This book does not often receive a lot of attention in sermons, worship, and Bible study, yet I am most grateful for its existence within our Christian canon. Lamentations is a book of deep emotions stemming from a painful,

54. Ibid., 43.
55. Ibid., 44.
56. Ibid., 78.

faith-shattering crisis between the Jewish community and God. How could God allow or bring about such atrocities? Though God is addressed throughout the five chapters of this book that expresses pain, fury and despair, God never responds within the framework of this literature.

Noted biblical scholar Kathleen O'Conner suggests, "God never responds in Lamentations, but the book itself becomes a comforting witness. It is a 'house of sorrow' and a safe place for tears. It honors the voices of loss, pain, and despair. It mirrors pain back to those who suffer and, in the process, brings them out of isolation into community, even if only briefly . . . Lamentations is about the collapse of a physical, emotional, and spiritual universe of an entire people, not about individual sorrows except in a meta-phoric and symbolic manner. Yet the power of its poetry can embrace the sufferings of any whose bodies and spirits are worn down and assaulted, whose boundaries have shrunk, who are trapped, and now face foreclosed futures."[57]

Another Lamentations scholar, F. W. Dobbs-Allsopp notes, "however dark life must have been for the post-destruction community of Jerusalem and its surrounding environs, it is a fitting tribute to this community's resilience that the one literary work that can be attributed to its members most securely, the sequence of the five poems collected . . . is a most profoundly life-embracing work . . . Lamentations may well be the most remarkable and compelling testament to the human spirit's will to live in all of the Old Testament."[58]

Historical Context and Literary Features

Lamentations arose in the aftermath of a truly cataclysmic event in Jewish history. In 536 BCE, Jerusalem and the Holy Temple were destroyed by a Babylonian invasion. God's "chosen people" who once believed that God would never abandon them and keep safe

---

57. O'Conner, *Lamentations and the Tears of the World*, xiii–xiv.

58. Dobbs-Allsopp, *Lamentations*, 2.

their holy city and temple, now looked upon total destruction. The siege by Nebuchadnezzar's armies lasted nearly two years, thus trapping the citizens inside the walled, isolated city as they suffered from famine. Eventually the Babylonian forces broke through and those who survived the onslaught were either carried off to Babylon or left in the region to pick up the pieces of a broken life.

Even though it is probably true that the rest of the region outside Jerusalem witnessed a remarkable degree of continuity in material culture, the catastrophic event should not be minimized nor should the terribleness of that community's lived reality be misread. Judah had lost its national independence and was forced to live under foreign domination and persecution. In a span of about fifteen years there were three successive deportations and its cumulative effects took its toll on a once proud people.[59] The survivors would have been numbed by years of violence and deaths by family members. The poems could have come out of any one of these invasions.[60] Despite the fact that tradition often links authorship to Jeremiah, there is no concrete evidence for this. However, the books of Jeremiah and Lamentations originated in the same general historical period, and so the attribution of his authorship may rest in the ancient custom of designating works to well-known personages.[61]

The principle literary form of this book is the lament; prayers of the discontented, the disturbed, and the distraught. "Lamentations adapts the typical lament form by leaving out features in a signal of its own purposes . . . They reduce or omit features expressing confident hope, assurance, and praise, and they greatly expand the complaints. Discontent and disorientation abound in the very structure of the poetry itself."[62] These five poems draw upon both individual and communal laments, as well as city laments and

59. Ibid., 1–2.

60. O'Conner, *Lamentations and the Tears of the World*, 7.

61. Dobbs-Allsopp, *Lamentations*, 5.

62. O'Conner, *Lamentations and the Tears of the World*, 9–10.

funeral dirges. The dirge proclaims a death, announces a funeral, and summons the community to mourn.[63]

The city lament genre is best known from ancient Mesopotamia in which the destruction of particular cities and their most important shrines are depicted. The destruction is brought about by the divine assembly and the abandonment of its chief gods,[64] yet "Lamentations is no simple Mesopotamian city lament. Rather, it represents a thorough translation and adaptation of the genre in a Judean environment and is ultimately put to a significantly different use...Lamentations employs structural and rhetorical devices well known to Hebrew poetry. In Lamentations the people are held responsible for the destruction of Jerusalem because of their sin, whereas in the Mesopotamian laments the destruction is attributed to the capricious decision of the divine assembly."[65] However, the most striking difference is the complete absence in Lamentations of any mention of God's return to Jerusalem or the restoration of the city and temple.[66] This motif is perhaps one of the greatest characteristics of the Mesopotamian city lament since it ultimately looks forward to the restoration and rebuilding of city and temples, and the resumption of normalcy for the larger community.

Literarily, Lamentations is comprised of four acrostic poems and one "alphabetic" poem. "An acrostic is a composition that begins with the first letter of the alphabet and uses the rest of the letters sequentially. Each verse of the Lamentations' acrostics begins with consecutive letters of the Hebrew alphabet, but, adding complexity to the poetry, the acrostics vary in length and type. The final poem is 'alphabetic' in the sense that it contains twenty-two lines, the same number of lines as the number of consonants in the Hebrew alphabet."[67]

---

63. Ibid., 10.

64. Dobbs-Allsopp, *Lamentations*, 7.

65. Ibid., 9.

66. Ibid., 10.

67. O'Conner, *Lamentations and the Tears of the World*, 11.

O'Conner asks, why does Lamentations use acrostic and alphabetic forms? She suggests, "the alphabetic devices embody struggles of survivors to contain and control the chaos of unstructured pain . . . To write an acrostic is difficult in any language, requiring verbal fluency beyond demands of ordinary poetry. Lamentations' acrostics indicate that the poems are not spontaneous outbursts but carefully composed works."[68] Furthermore she contends, "Lamentations' alphabetic devices are deeply symbolic. They expose the depth and breadth of suffering in conflicting ways. The alphabet gives both order and shape to suffering that is otherwise inherently chaotic, formless, and out of control. It signifies the enormity of suffering as a vast universe of pain, extending from 'A to Z' . . . It implies that suffering is infinite, for it spans the basic components of written language from beginning to end."[69]

Another distinctive feature of Lamentations is that it contains multiple testimonies and voices among survivors; no one speaker dominates the other. "The book leaves voices and viewpoints unsettled, unresolved, and open-ended . . . Together the voices express complex and uneven processes of coping with trauma in which hope flares up and fades."[70] One such voice found in the first and second chapters is the "Daughter of Zion." "By making Jerusalem a woman, the poetry gives her personality and human characteristics that evoke pity or disdain from the readers. Her female body is the object of disgrace and shaming, and her infidelities become shocking, intimate betrayals."[71] As mentioned earlier, one voice that we expect to hear from is God's, but we do not. All the book's speakers agree that God must respond to them in their suffering, but God's voice goes unheard and is missing. With this silence "Lamentations expresses human experiences of abandonment with full force. And because God never speaks, the

68. Ibid., 12.
69. Ibid., 13.
70. Ibid., 14.
71. Ibid., 14.

book honors voices of pain. Lamentations is a house for sorrow because there is not speech for God."[72]

Chapters 1-5

Chapter 1 opens this book with two voices having equal opportunity to speak: the narrator and Daughter Zion. The narrator opens the chapter with a funeral over the city and is unmoved by the pain as he describes the losses experienced by Daughter Zion. Losses include those of power, wealth, honor, status, security, inhabitants, temple, and a lack of a comforter; he also blames her for her sinful ways. Daughter Zion, however, is full of emotion as she describes the loss of her children and her present pain. She is overwhelmed by the horror and trauma of her rape. Although she acknowledges her sin that results in destruction, her greatest loss is that no one is there to comfort her, particularly God. Throughout the chapter she begs God to look at her, pay attention, and see what the enemy has done to her, but God does not reply. Eventually she weeps because of God's awful treatment of her. "Like most survivors of trauma, Daughter Zion cannot get a hearing . . . When she finds words for her pain, she cannot get a hearing. There is no one to comfort her."[73]

The second chapter contains the same two voices as the first, but the narrator dominates the speaking; Daughter Zion speaks only the last three verses. The significance of this chapter is that the narrator has moved from being an objective describer of events to being an emotional comforter of Zion's suffering who now joins in on the lament. He too begins to hurl accusations at God, charging God with violent abuse of Zion.[74] "For the narrator, God's cruel actions contradict God's own interests. God violated God's special relationship with Zion, destroyed God's own dwelling place, and ended worship in the temple that celebrated and sealed that

72. Ibid., 15.
73. Ibid., 29.
74. Ibid., 33.

relationship."[75] The narrator now stands with Daughter Zion, in spite of her own self-confessed sins, and now speaks directly to her. However, as he decries the abuse, he also blames the prophets and religious leadership for Zion's downfall, as well as passersby and Zion's enemies. Though he does not intercede for her, he appeals to Daughter Zion to speak out on behalf of her lost children. She again begs God to see her and the devastation, but again God offers no response. However, unlike chapter 1, she has now gained a witness and compassionate advocate in the narrator. She is barely heard from again in this book.

The next chapter introduces a new anonymous voice: "the strongman." This speaker is a captive and testifies to the pain from that experience, and perhaps also serves as a metaphorical voice of the people. Like Daughter Zion, he too struggles to find a witness of his anguish and calls out to God to look at his plight. However, in the midst of his complaints of rejection and suffering he briefly articulates hope and recalls God's faithfulness. But it soon dissipates as he is so engulfed in his own trauma. The poem struggles with the conflict between divine rejection and divine mercy.[76] Both times in chapter 3 when the strongman voices a glimmer of hope, he is at rock bottom with no place else to go. This inexplicable hope "emerges without clear cause like grace, without explanation . . . The strongman's hope is unsteady; it comes, goes, and comes again repeatedly."[77]

Chapter 4 offers a chance for two more voices to speak who both appear hopeless and exhausted: an unidentified narrator and the people. In the first part of the chapter, the narrator (probably a different one than from chapter 1) takes the reader on a tour of the city after the invasion. His tone is observational and uninvolved, and "his words sweep across the destruction, letting it speak for itself in its depravity and deprivation."[78] After suggesting some blame to Zion and her mothers, he points his finger to the commu-

75. Ibid., 34.
76. Ibid., 51.
77. Ibid., 57.
78. Ibid., 59.

nity leaders as the responsible ones for God's anger that resulted in this national catastrophe. But like previous chapters, the narrator suggests that God no longer pays attention to the people and the leaders have become invisible from God's sight. The people is the speaker in the second half of the chapter. This speaker offers the first words in Lamentations of the actual destruction and invasion, not simply the aftermath as the other speakers did.[79] This voice never once speaks to God or demands anything from God. Rather, the poem ends by the people gloating over the future pain of its enemies. O'Conner states, "Hatred and wishes for vengeance against cruel and oppressive enemies are typical and normal human responses to trauma. The ethical dilemma appears when people begin to act upon those desires. This poem brings the community's response into the open, creating psychic and spiritual space to begin imagining another reality, a different future."[80]

Chapter 5 continues with the voice of the people as a long petition that urges, insists, and demands God's attention. As a reader, one would hope that God might finally offer salvation and rescue. Even in the end of this chapter and book, the people have turned to God, as was done throughout Lamentations, and want the relationship with God restored. They are waiting for God to make the next move. "But in this 'house of sorrow' no happy ending awaits the occupants. Grief and anger, doubt and despair have taken up residence and will not be evicted."[81] This Hebrew poem ends very different than other Mesopotamian city laments which usually end by the gods returning to the city and restoring it. Lamentations ends in tragedy and there is still no answer from God.[82] Structurally, this poem is much shorter and less structured than the first four chapters. O'Conner suggests, "Its diminished length and abandonment of the acrostic imply a numbing, recurring despair among survivors and leave the book without closure.

---

79. Ibid., 66.
80. Ibid., 69.
81. Ibid., 70.
82. Dobbs-Allsopp, *Lamentations*, 141.

But that refusal of resolution enable the book in its turbulence, conflict, and confusion to portray pain without compromise."[83]

Embodying Lamentations Today

What is a person to make of Lamentations? What is the good news in this message? How are we to incorporate this book of pain and rejection into our personal faith life and into our faith community? Lamentations is a book of truth-telling, even if it is quite raw and explicit. Lamentations invites companionship in ways similar to how the narrator responded to Daughter Zion in the two opening chapters. Furthermore, pastoral theologian Jaco Hamman contends, "The Book of Lamentations refuses denial, practices truth-telling, and reverses any amnesia, whether in the lives of individuals or in Gospel communities. It invites readers into communal and individual suffering. It sensitizes one to the pain that is present in the world . . . The truth-telling of Lamentations's theology of witness offers hope for the body of Christ and comfort for a world that knows pain and suffering intimately."[84]

Lamentations enables various voices to speak up. However, one voice is missing—God's. For some reason, God does not speak or respond or heal or "see." O'Conner suggests that the silence of God is inspired. It shows "a brilliant restraint that breathes power into the book. If God were to speak, what would God say? . . . God's speechlessness in Lamentations must be a calculated choice, a conscious theological decision, an inspired control by the book's composers, for how could a response from the deity do anything but ruin the book? . . . No matter what God said, Lamentations would come to premature resolution, and the book's capacity to house sorrow would dissipate. Any words from God would endanger human voices."[85]

83. O'Conner, *Lamentations and the Tears of the World*, 71.

84. Hamman, *When Steeples Cry*, 120.

85. O'Conner, *Lamentations and the Tears of the World*, 85.

In other words, there is a time for appropriate silence when dealing with excruciating and intense pain. No words are able to comfort the soul. However, the mere presence of someone can be a source of strength and encouragement. Though the voices in this book suggest that God does not look at their suffering, the reality is that this canonical book is a cry for help and therefore some level of faith must have existed that God was listening. This book honors truth-telling because God receives these words and does not retaliate or get defensive.

The overall witness of this book denies denial, but instead "urges readers to face suffering, to speak of it, to be dangerous proclaimers of the truths that nations, families, and individuals prefer to repress. They invite us to honor the pain muffled in our hearts, overlooked in our society, and crying for our attention in other parts of the world."[86] It calls forth naming the suffering rather than hiding it or pretending that it does not exist, and thereby begins the healing process by giving speech to pain. The lament found in Lamentations is of extreme nature, and thereby offers a holy resource to people who too are suffering extreme trauma, pain, and loss.

Lamentations invites us to become compassionate advocates for those who suffer. The narrator in the first two chapters began as an objective, unmoved person to one who also emotionally cried out about the tragedy after hearing the cries of Daughter Zion and seeing the first-hand accounts of suffering and destruction. He gave her room to speak and thus validated her story. Eventually he was so moved that he altered the way he saw the world and God, and entered into the lament. Today, we too are called to open our eyes to the suffering around us. In doing so, we too may be transformed as we compassionately walk with those who hurt.

Though this book is one of extreme lament, there are glimpses of hope found within it. Unfortunately, as soon as the hope surfaces it then seems to vanish. This may be true to life for many of us who have suffered a great loss; some days are better and more positive than other days. We are not the first ones to experience

86. Ibid., 95.

such grief. The words of this book affirm our up-and-down-ness. Furthermore, it also acknowledges that in our extreme pain, others dare not inappropriately "push us" out of our despair faster than we are able. If they truly want to be compassionate advocates, they will need to offer the space to allow the grief to go as it pleases. Yes, some days may seem hopeful, but we should not be discouraged when those dark days also set in again.

Liturgical and devotional use of Lamentations also has its place within our churches. It is a prayer of brokenness stemming from utter brokenness, and so therefore it can teach us how to pray.[87] The main genre found in this book is that of lament, though it does push it beyond the traditional form and range of anger and despair. Ultimately, the book reaches to God over and over again, even in the face of extreme pain. We are to persistently reach to God in our own pain as well, which summons us to reach beyond ourselves. There is much pain and trauma in this world. We too are invited to pray and reach out to God on behalf of others so that shalom may prevail. In this way it serves as an example of intercessory prayer in the work for peace and reconciliation.

Conclusion

For the sake of the Gospel and its relevance to our world today, biblical lament needs to be a fundamental aspect of our Christian faith. Leaders must assist people in engaging this expression of faith for both personal devotions and corporate worship settings. We will need to take steps in recovering aspects of this for our faith. Patrick Miller suggests, " . . . the Christian community learns about the place and practice of lament from attending to the voices of lament."[88] He proposes three voices from which we hear the sounds of lament: the human voice, the voice of Christ, and the voice of the world.

---

87. Ibid., 124.
88. Miller, "Heaven's Prisoners," 15.

The voice of the human cries to God for help in the midst of injustice and suffering, which is consistent throughout the whole of scripture. "This is indeed the primary mode of conversation between God and the human creature . . . The lament, therefore, is not exceptional. It is the rule."[89] Lament not only is the voice of pain, but it is also the voice of prayer. No matter how painful and raw and explicit our lament is, this prayer of help stemming from our innermost being assumes that God is there, can be present, and can help. At the heart of this prayer is the paradoxical conjoining of question and trust, of protest and acceptance, of fear and confidence as we seek to persuade God to act.[90] As we consider lament for today, we may need to learn again how to ask for God's help in times of trouble and woe.

The voice of Christ recalls the utterances of Jesus on the cross. Not only does his cry to God of lament bless our own engagement with biblical lament, it also offers us an "understanding [of] *the work of God* in Jesus Christ, for it is our chief clue that Christ died not simply as one *of* us but also as one *for* us, both *with* us and *in our behalf* . . . Jesus died for our *suffering* as much as for our *sins*."[91] Jesus' words from the cross continue to teach us today how to pray and that it is okay to place our doubts and despair into God's hands. Suffering is not the last word. And, we are to cry out on behalf of the suffering of others.[92]

The voice of the world calls us as Christ's followers to give attention to it. Christ listened to the pain and suffering of those around him, cried out to God on their behalf, and responded in appropriate ways. Praying the prayers of Christ help us to better discern the laments of this world and offer solidarity to our neighbor.[93] Laments are prayers for help and for justice.

As we seek to faithfully respond to Christ's call in this world, praying our own laments and attuning ourselves to the work of

89. Ibid., 16.
90. Ibid., 19.
91. Ibid., 21.
92. Ibid., 22–23.
93. Ibid., 23–24.

Christ will sharpen our ears to the suffering around us. Recovering lament in our faith will guide us through not only our own abandonment issues and times of forsakenness, but also foster a more sympathetic and understanding posture to friends, family, and others facing similar situations of vulnerability and pain. But this compassionate stance is merely the first step in more active expressions of intercession and response to the needs. For too long our American society has emphasized success and decried suffering and loss as signs of failure. It is time that we Christians strive for faithfulness rather than "success" that denies, hides, and oppresses. Engaging practices of biblical lament matures our faithfulness to Christ's call and Gospel.

3

Writing Your Own Prayer of Lament

O Lord, why have you forsaken me in my time of need?

Do you not love me like you say you do?

Why have you not comforted me?

You should have helped me in my time of need!

I remember when you talked with me in my prayers.

I remember when you walked with me in my mind.

You have healed me oh Lord with your wonderful word of encouragement,

you have helped me through my time of need oh Lord.

—JUNIOR HIGH ADOLESCENT

Lord, why am I this way? Why do you allow me to cause myself to sin and suffer?

Why do I sin? Why do I force evil thoughts into my head?

Why do my friends suffer so much and cause them to sin and hurt themselves?

Thank you Lord for helping me through my tough time when

I was cutting and punishing myself.

You are truly the most high God and lead me to the end.

—MALE, HIGH SCHOOL ADOLESCENT

Why, O Lord, do I keep running into the same walls?

I feel as though somehow I let me down, or is it really that I feel you let me down.

Lead me through this frustration, help me to remember your goodness.

To remember that you were the good of all those who are called according to your purposes.

Help me to praise you, you lift me up and I do praise you.

Thank you, God for your goodness and second chances.

—EMERGING ADULT

THE PREVIOUS THREE PRAYERS are examples of laments that I collected as part of a project I conducted in 2006 with several churches. Engaging practices of lament may take many forms in both individual and corporate settings. For this project, I invited several pastors to lead their youth and young adults in a three-step, six-minute, timed-writing prayer exercise in which they wrote their own laments. I also led this exercise in one of my college youth ministry classes. Though participants wrote their own individual prayers of lament, they did so in a group context. In other words, these are personal laments but written during a corporate experience. In this chapter, I will outline this particular prayer practice and offer some observations from this project.

The Project

The three Mennonite congregations who participated in this project were all from Indiana, though from different towns. The first congregation had an average attendance of two hundred thirty attendees and was set in a town with a population of 3,200; most church-goers lived within a fifteen minute radius of the church. The second was a rural congregation with an average attendance of two hundred; the building was located among cornfields. The third congregation had an average attendance of three hundred fifty and located in a small city with a population of 32,000. The fourth setting was one of my college youth ministry classes where most of the students were in their late teens or early twenties; not all of these students were Mennonite.

I prepared the pastors to lead their respective adolescent groups by helping them better understand biblical lament, its role in faith development and pastoral care of adolescents, and instructing them in ways they could lead their groups in this specific prayer practice. They were invited to lead this exercise up to four times over a period of six months. I then collected an assortment of data from the youth leaders, including about one hundred thirty prayers written by youth and responses by youth to questionnaires following the first and fourth times this exercise was done.

The first questionnaire asked the following: Have you ever prayed a prayer of lament before?; Was it comfortable or uncomfortable to do this type of praying? Why or how so?; What did you enjoy most about this way of praying?; What did you least enjoy about this way of praying?; Do you think your friends, other than those in your youth group, would enjoy this prayer exercise? Why or why not?; Do you think your family members or other adults that you know would enjoy this prayer exercise? Why or why not?

The second questionnaire asked the following: How many times have you done this prayer exercise in the past few months?; What did you enjoy most about this way of praying?; What did you least enjoy about this way of praying?; Are there any particular challenges that made this way of praying difficult for you?; Are there particular joys that made this way of praying rewarding for you?; How has this type of prayer helped or hindered your relationship with God? the church?

The Prayer Exercise

As previously stated, my goal was to have these various adolescent groups write their own prayer of lament on four different occasions through a specific timed-writing exercise. I wanted to examine how early, middle, and late adolescents would engage a practice of lament on a routine basis, rather than solely in times of extreme crisis. I had hoped that by having adolescents participate in this form of lament, their faith would be positively impacted and would encourage them and their leaders to more regularly engage in practices of biblical lament. Finally, because I believed there was a gap in the knowledge of biblical lament among churchgoers, I had hoped that by participating in this project that more pastoral leaders would be educated about this body of biblical literature and its function in faith development.

The idea for this three-step, six-minute prayer exercise came to me a few years prior when I read the chapter "Grieving" in *Way to Live: Christian Practices for Teens*, edited by Dorothy Bass and Don Richter. The first step invites youth to spend two minutes addressing their anger and pain towards God by pouring out their written, raw emotions. The second step invites them to devote two minutes remembering and writing about a time of God's goodness and faithfulness in their lives, or an occasion when they knew that God heard them. The third step welcomes youth to then write for two minutes their praises and thanksgivings to God.

Before the young people engaged this prayer practice for the first time, I encouraged the leaders to introduce the concept of biblical lament to them by reviewing a handout found at the end of this chapter. Psalm 13 served as an example of lament. To be sure, the three-step pattern is a simplified view of the technical intricacies found in many biblical laments. However, this contains most of the key elements found within many biblical laments. I encouraged the pastors to create a safe space and environment for this activity. Though youth were invited to engage in this prayer exercise, they would also know that they could "pass" at any time with any aspects of this corporate experience.

Furthermore, youth were told that this three-step exercise should not be treated as a "magic formula" where their deep pains could be "cured" in six simple minutes. The reality is that we simply do not know how long it took the biblical writers to craft their laments. Did it take them weeks or months or even years to get from step 1 to step 3? For me this is grace that we do not know. Therefore, it is acceptable if it takes time to actually move through these various steps in life. Perhaps it is more authentic for me to "hang out" in step 1 before I can actually write about step 2 depending the issue that is on my heart and mind.

Each time the pastors began this prayer exercise, I instructed them to light a candle, offer an opening prayer, or perform some other ritualistic activity that let youth know "Now we begin." Then after they engaged the three-step writing exercise for six minutes, I encouraged leaders to engage in one of the following optional activities, depending on the group's comfort level. Youth could read their prayer aloud to the rest of the group or to a partner beside them. Or, they could all pass in their prayers to the leader to be anonymously read aloud to the group. Again, I stressed to the leaders that young people could "pass" on turning in or reading aloud their prayers since this was to be a safe place for them to honestly engage God. To conclude the actual worship experience, I instructed the leaders to extinguish the candle, offer a concluding prayer, or do some other ritualistic activity that let youth know "Now we are finished."

There was one other optional way of engaging this form of lament I encouraged the pastors to try as the group became more comfortable with this practice. Instead of this being a solo writing experience, youth could partner with another group member to write a joint lament. This would foster conversation between the two before they would agree on what was to be written. Other than my own class doing this one time, none of the other pastors attempted this option.

Project Observations

The following observations from this project are divided into categories of early, middle, and late adolescence, as well as pastor reflections. My intent is to offer a summarized overview of the project, not a detailed analysis.

Early Adolescence

Most junior highers were comfortable praying this way and simply appreciated the opportunity to express their emotions to God. This demonstrates the importance of engaging young people not only with this prayer of lament, but also in setting aside times to engage with other prayer disciplines that invite reflection. However, I note two issues that surfaced from the questionnaires. First, there were some who struggled to know if it was okay to argue with God; but, some of the "struggle" was connected to this being a new experience for them. Second, a high percentage of these youth had not previously engaged in any form of biblical lament that they were aware. This exemplifies the biblical illiteracy of lament in these Christian settings. Simply engaging this practice on a regular basis will educate youth about biblical lament and provide for them a resource for when life's tough circumstances arise. From the voluntarily submitted written prayers of lament, three common themes emerged: school, friendships, and family. Overall, these prayers of lament reflected the current "everydayness" of life rather than some past, major crisis event. I will also note that I did not observe any differences between girls and boys in their ability and willingness to engage this practice; both genders equally participated.

Though this project was geared toward youth, there were some adult sponsors who completed the questionnaires. One adult noted her appreciation for this prayer exercise because it made her feel better and closer to God after writing down her emotions. But, she also indicated that at times it was difficult to know what to write about and that it "seem[ed] unnatural to argue with God."

Middle Adolescence

Just like the early adolescents, an overwhelming majority of senior highers appreciated the opportunity to vent and express their honest emotions to God. And, a higher number of them stated that this series of prayer exercises actually helped their relationship with God and the church. The middle adolescents valued knowing that God wanted them to be true in their words, which is a step beyond simply appreciating the opportunity. They were able to theologically understand and appreciate that God's very being is one who yearns for an authentic, intimate relationship with people.

Nevertheless, there was still a significant minority of middle adolescents who found it difficult to actually argue with God at first. A few questioned the theological appropriateness, yet most comfortably engaged this mode of praying the first time they did it and throughout. However, it should be mentioned that a few of these youth did not enjoy writing their prayers. Even though they were not opposed to engaging biblical lament, some struggled with writing as a mode of prayer.

As with the early adolescents, middle adolescents were given the opportunity to voluntarily turn in their written laments. Compared to the younger age group, these prayers were more abstract in nature and did not engage the "everydayness" of life to the same degree. Some wrote about sin, human greed, divine abandonment, and human suffering. But, there were still a significant number of prayers that touched on the everyday realities of life, including struggles with relationships (peer, family, romantic), personal afflictions, loneliness, frustration with their bodies and minds, stress, family suffering, and yearning for a sense of direction in life.

Late Adolescence

Similar to the previous two age groups, late adolescents over-whelmingly enjoyed the space and structure to vent their problems and express their feelings to God. In some ways, this could validate that their lives are too busy and do not have adequate time for reflection and stillness. One person commented, "The idea of being angry with God seemed a little odd at first, but then realizing that I don't have to protect God . . . just to be reverent and honest in my approach." One person expressed that they had been taught that such a view of blaming God was a negative approach to dealing with problems. Another said that they do not like to blame God because there is too much to be grateful. And another indicated that they and God were not on the "best of terms right now," so steps 2 and 3 (remembering of God's faithfulness, praising God) were difficult to do. Still others expressed that this mode of prayer felt more like a dialogue with God and valued that both anger and praise could be expressed. A significant number stated that they recalled certain painful memories or frustrations that they thought were resolved. Some confessed that seeing their vulnerable emotions on paper in an "exposing" way "dug" at their pain.

As with the junior and senior highers, I was not able to determine any significant difference among young adult males and females in their responses to the questionnaires. And like the previous age groups, there was a significantly high percentage of young people who believed their family, friends, and peers would enjoy this way of praying. I believe this suggests a yearning and receptivity for this type of faith practice not only among younger people, but for all age groups.

The actual writing of their prayers was a hindrance for a small minority of late adolescents. They desired more time for reflection than the allotted six minutes. From their written prayers, two major content themes arose: yearning for a deeper intimacy with God and seeking greater clarity in vocational direction. Issues of human suffering (familial, global), responsibility and stress were other themes that emerged, but to a lesser degree. The prayers among late adolescents seemed to exemplify general developmental struggles among this age group.

Pastor Reflections

The final component of data collection involved a lunch meeting with the two youth pastors who led their youth groups in this project; the third youth pastor was unable to attend. Both pastors enthusiastically embraced the need to engage their youth in practices of biblical lament, and plan to continue some version of this in the future. Both agreed that they were now more knowledgeable of the structure and understanding of biblical lament, and better equipped to work out of a pastoral care framework of lament when crises or needs may arise. For example, one pastor revealed that since her group began these exercises, one of the girls experienced a particular crisis. Now as a pastor, she can use biblical lament as a personal resource. The other pastor mentioned that since his groups engaged these practices, a parent, who was also a volunteer adult sponsor, separated from her husband. They had three children; two were in the senior high and junior high youth groups. He was considering how he might use biblical lament to help the entire youth group deal with this painful situation.

Both pastors affirmed the structural flow of how biblical lament eventually leads to praise of God. The complaints of the psalmists are not mere ends in and of themselves. These prayers are honestly directed to God. However, both acknowledged that it was important to not rush youth through the three steps. For example, one pastor shared that one of the girls in her youth group has been "stuck" in step 1 (arguing with God) and had yet to make it to steps 2 or 3 (remembrance of God's goodness, praise of God). Though this pastor wondered at times if this "stuckness" may actually not benefit this middle adolescent, I reminded her that there is one psalm that "begins in the pit and ends in the pit" (Psalm 88). And, that Lamentations is an example of an extreme form of biblical lament in which God does not speak nor seem to offer comfort.

These two leaders agreed that one hurdle to overcome for the youth was to simply know what to lament about. Sometimes, youth were not feeling frustrated or angry or had previously vented their laments. I asked them, if in those times either one had encouraged their youth to lament on behalf of someone else, thus functioning as a form of intercessory prayer. Neither one had, but both thought that would be a good idea. One pastor pointed out that a short time before her youth did their final prayer of lament, she had led a Bible study on "needs" and "hungers" of the world. A high number of her youth lamented global poverty and material excesses found in America. The other pastor noted that some of the participants simply had trouble writing because they struggled with some learning disabilities. He wondered if I had ever had people do something other than writing. I told him that at times I had encouraged people to draw their laments as one way to engage more of our senses. Other possibilities include sculpting, molding clay, painting, writing music, or other artistic means. (For more variations, see chapter 6.)

Through this experience of engaging their adolescents with biblical lament, both pastors were convinced of its importance. A few years ago the one pastor first prayed this same timed-writing prayer exercise of lament at a youth pastor retreat. He said that it was done at the end of the day and it enabled him to process some of the pain and problems that welled up inside him throughout the day. But now that he has led it with early, middle, and late adolescents he continues to believe this to be a good faith practice for people. The other pastor also recognized the importance of engaging youth with biblical lament and made a comment that resonated with all three of us—"Pain sells." She was referring to an ad that she had seen in which the image was that of a painful subject used to sell a particular product. As we discussed the reality that many of our churches shy away from enabling people to vulnerably share their wounds, hurts, and scars with each other, she exclaimed, "If pain sells and churches don't offer a place, then no wonder the youth [and perhaps people of other ages as well] eventually leave the church!"

Conclusion

All three adolescent age groups appreciated the opportunity to express their honest emotions and feelings to God. The majority of the young people from these settings had not previously prayed a lament, but a high percentage of them were comfortable engaging this timed-writing prayer exercise. Many of these adolescents believed that their friends, family members, and older adults would enjoy this practice as well. This demonstrates a general hunger for people to vulnerably share in authentic and intimate ways, or at least a desire to offer to God their built-up emotions. Even though biblical lament practices may be new and different to many people in our society, I believe there is receptivity for such practices of lament. And in this way, such efforts will speak to the yearning for people to connect with God and others about their struggles, losses, and grievances.

Having read through the data of this project, including responses to the questionnaires, the voluntarily submitted prayers of lament, and a final evaluation meeting with two pastors who led their youth groups through this prayer practice, I am more convinced than before that engaging biblical lament is needed today. Not only is there a void of such faith practices in our American context, I believe that people will be receptive to it. However, it will take courageous pastoral leaders to guide people through these practices. If my final conversation with the two pastors is any indication of other pastors who may consider doing such prayer exercises with their youth groups, then this too will nurture their personal faith and professional development, and better equip them to walk with youth in their own realities of faith formation and pastoral care.

Prayers of Lament

"The practice of lament gives you time and permission to vent your pent-up anger, your deep sadness, and your self-blame. You allow yourself to grieve in a way that leads to healing and renewal. As you pour out your grief, loss, pain, and anger in the presence of God, you discover that God hears your cries of anguish and comforts you. While you can't remove the storms, quiet the thunder, or stop the lightning from striking, you can trust your tears to be the raindrops that release the clouds, allowing rays of sunlight to shine through. Before catching a glimpse of the rainbow, though, you have to brace yourself for the raging storm within."[1]

Prayer Exercise

Write your own "3-Act" psalm. It does not need to be long.

Act I: **Arguing with God**

> ☹ People get mad at God and pour out their raw emotions.

Act II: **Remembering God's goodness**

> ☺ Gradually those who complained to God remember God's help in the past and know that God has heard them.

Act III: **Praising God**

> ☺ Those who lament realize they can trust God with their lives and they tell God, "Thanks!"

1. Bass, Dorothy & Don Richter, eds. *Way to Live: Christian Practices for Teens.* (Nashville: Upper Room Books, 2002), page 251.

Psalm 13

[1] How long, O Lord? Will you forget me forever? How long will you hide your face from me? [2] How long must I bear pain in my soul, and have sorrow in my heart all day long? How long shall my enemy be exalted over me? [3] Consider and answer me, O Lord my God! Give light to my eyes, or I will sleep the sleep of death, [4] and my enemy will say, "I have prevailed"; my foes will rejoice because I am shaken. [5] But I trusted in your steadfast love; my heart shall rejoice in your salvation. [6] I will sing to the Lord, because he has dealt bountifully with me.

"Perhaps you are grieving a personal loss... Perhaps you are standing with others who are mourning the death of a loved one. The grief and other emotions you are experiencing are natural and inevitable. But when you glimpse the rainbow amid the storm, know that you are not alone. God is with you, and God can handle all the anger and cursing and complaints that your grief process provokes. You are surrounded by fellow sufferers who are also grieving loss; they will open their hearts to you and hold you up as you try to get your bearings again. Give yourself— and others—time and space to grieve in a way that leads to healing and renewal. That's what the practice of lament is all about."[2]

2. *Way to Live*, page 260.

4

The Role of Biblical Lament
in Pastoral Care of Adolescents

Why Lord have you left me? Why can't I feel your presence?

*You aren't there! You're not helping me or showing
love towards me!*

*I know you're there, though. You were there
in my many trials.*

In fact, you carried me during those trials!

*I have felt your presence and I knew you were there
helping and loving me.*

But I trust you. I know you are there.

Your love is great. I praise because you are a hand in need!

—FEMALE, SENIOR HIGH ADOLESCENT

It is often hard, oh Lord, to feel your guidance.

*I fail to see your footprints, and I don't see how
I can walk in your path.*

Where is your guiding beacon?

Where is your path through the wilderness?

*I clear my vision though, and I realize that
while I cannot see a path,*

I can feel your hand on my shoulder.

I embrace the fact that you have a purpose for me

*and rejoice in the fact that you have always pulled
me through.*

—YOUNG ADULT

THE PREVIOUS LAMENTS ARE examples of "the voice of the human/ adolescent" from the project described in chapter 3. They both express a lack of attention from God or an inability to feel God's presence in their life's journey. Such voices are all too common among adolescents today. Consider the following "voice of the adolescent world."

Suicide among teens has sharply increased in the past several decades[1] by 155 percent from 1962 to 1996, following car accidents and homicide.[2] The Centers for Disease Control and Prevention web site states, "Suicide is a serious public health problem that affects many young people. Suicide is the third leading cause of death for youth between the ages of 10 and 24, and results in approximately 4,600 lives lost each year...Suicide among teens and young adults has nearly tripled since the 1940's."[3] Self-mutilation and eating disorders among both girls and boys continues to rise.[4] Anorexia has been called "the underground prophet in our midst."[5]

1. Rowatt, Jr., *Adolescents in Crisis*, 147; Elkind, *The Hurried Child*, xvii.

2. Parrott III, *Helping the Struggling Adolescent*, 430; Elkind, *The Hurried Child*, 18.

3. Centers for Disease Control and Prevention, "Suicide Among Youth," lines 1–3, 9.

4. Parrott, *Helping the Struggling Adolescent*, 139; Atkinson, *Ministry with Youth in Crisis*, 213.

5. Grinenko Baker, *Doing Girlfriend Theology*, 158.

Today's young people experience significant loss and instability due to parental divorce. In 1940 the divorce rate affected 2 percent of the married population, but as of 2002 43 percent of first-time marriages end in separation or divorce within fifteen years of marriage.[6] The definition of "family" continues to evolve with blended family situations.

As stated in chapter 1, adolescence is a time when young people struggle for a sense of identity and belonging. Who will they be when they "grow up"? What vocation will they embrace? Whose influential voices will they claim as their loyalty? As various personal and societal pressures abound, young people will be involved in and face significant change in a short span of years. As adult Christian caregivers, what is our role in accompanying them through this time of life? More importantly as it relates to this book, how can the role of biblical lament be claimed as an appropriate function of pastoral care?

In this chapter, I will consider the various voices of lament, particularly the voice of the adolescent and the voice of their reality, and suggest reasons for why engaging practices of biblical lament will enable adult spiritual caregivers to better offer pastoral care to adolescents. First, I will offer a brief overview of the adolescent journey and then explore various cultural and societal pressures which impact our young people. Then, I will then provide some images to help understand adolescent development, examine the effects of trauma on adolescent development, explain two types of crises adolescents face, and give particular attention to early, middle, and late adolescence. Finally, I will explore key pastoral care themes of resilience and hope.

Overview of the Adolescent Journey

Adolescence is a period in life that involves many changes for young people as they search for and discover personal identity and meaning. Physically, their bodies are changing as they mature

6. Clark, *Hurt 2.0*, 16.

from childhood to adulthood. Sexually, they are now able to reproduce even if psychologically they may not be prepared for such responsibilities. Socially, they may wander through various groups of friends, peers, and support networks. A junior higher changes friends as they move onto high school and engage in different school-sponsored activities. High schoolers graduate and form new friendships in college or other post-high life scenarios. As adolescents mature in their sense of personal identity, they will navigate religious beliefs, moral and ethical positions, and other intellectual ponderings.

"Adolescence" stems from a Latin word meaning "to grow up." Developmental psychologist John Santrock said "adolescence begins in biology and ends in culture."[7] The beginning of adolescence may be easier to determine than its ending since the onset of puberty is often linked to the start of it. There is still debate about this since physiological changes generally occur sooner in girls than in boys. A girl's first period is a clear distinction even though its onset is slowly dropping in age from an average of fourteen and a half years a century ago to eleven years today.[8] In boys, however, comparable physiological changes appear more gradual over time.

Nevertheless, the beginning of adolescence may be easier to trace than its ending. At what age does a person officially become a "grown up" and accept the responsibilities of adulthood? Is it sixteen when a person is able to obtain a driver's license, or eighteen when they become eligible to vote and join the military? Or is it twenty-one when they reach the legal age for alcohol consumption? One reason for the uncertainty of when adolescence is completed is that there are no clear, definitive markers of entering adulthood in the United States.

Richard Dunn suggests in his book *Shaping the Spiritual Life of Students: A Guide for Youth Workers, Pastors, Teachers, and Campus Ministers* there are three developmental sub-phases of adolescence: early (ages 10-14), middle (ages 13-19), and late (ages 18-25?). Rather than look to an "age of adolescent completion,"

7. Clark, "The Changing Face of Adolescence," 45.

8. Ibid., 45.

Dunn suggests there are four critical components of personal growth that must be integrated into a late adolescent's inner world before successful entrance into adulthood: intimate companionship, a compelling life vision, a coherent worldview, and a composition of commitments.[9] Sharon Daloz Parks suggests that the key marker that defines the task of the "young or emerging adult era" is "the birth of critical awareness and consequently in the dissolution and recomposition of the meaning of self, other, world, and 'God'"[10] as they self-consciously participate in an ongoing dialogue toward truth and cultivate a capacity to respond in ways that are satisfying and just.[11] However, Daloz Parks is more inclined to consider emerging adulthood as a post-adolescent period of life rather than viewing it as some form of "prolonged adolescence." Similarly, psychologist Jeffrey Arnett utilizes the term "emerging adult" to describe the period following adolescence and limits the term "adolescence" to junior high and high school age groups. Arnett describes five distinguishing features of emerging adulthood. It is the age of identify exploration, instability, self-focus, feeling in-between, and possibilities.[12] Though I believe that Dunn, Daloz Parks, and Arnett express similar sentiments, Daloz Parks contends that "there is a distinctive emerging adult way of making meaning in the often murky and overlooked territory between conventional faith (adolescence) and critical-systemic faith (adulthood)."[13]

Having offered a brief overview of some key realities of the adolescent journey, one can imagine there is much change during these years from ages eleven to thirty! But, is all change the same for each young person? Do they experience the adolescent journey in the same way? How do external forces and pressures influence development? What happens when life-altering losses occur, such

---

9. Dunn, *Shaping the Spiritual Life of Students*, 209.

10. Daloz Parks, *Big Questions, Worthy Dreams*, 8.

11. Ibid., 9.

12. Arnett, *Emerging Adulthood*, 8.

13. Daloz Parks, *Big Questions, Worthy Dreams*, 12.

as the death of a parent, loss of a limb, or other significant blows? How does this shape "normal" adolescent maturation?

Adolescent Cultural Landscapes

Hurried Children

In the preface of the third edition of his book *The Hurried Child: Growing Up Too Fast Too Soon*, child developmentalist David Elkind argues that children in the past few decades have been driven to grow up faster than what is appropriate. "Parents are under more pressure than ever to overschedule their children and have them engage in organized sports and other activities that may be age-inappropriate. Unhappily, the overtesting of children in public schools has become more extensive . . . The marketing of violence to children and youth has increased . . . The entertainment industry deliberately disregards its own ratings system and markets violent music, movies and video games directly to underage children."[14]

Even in his second edition of this book in 1988, Elkind argued, "The truth is that children in contemporary America, including advantaged children, are less well off today than they were a couple of decades ago."[15] Statistically, the infant mortality rate was increasing after a century of decline; more children lived in poverty than the previous two decades; there was a 50 percent increase in obesity among children and youth over the previous two decades; teenage pregnancy rates were the highest of any Western society and more than twice those of the next closest country; SAT scores had plummeted; and millions of children were being medicated, a several-hundred-fold increase over the previous five years.

Overall, Elkind argues that our society hurries children in ways that lead to an overabundant level of stress.[16] Normally when a person undergoes a high level of stress, there is adequate time to replenish one's energy reservoirs. But the pace and pressures

14. Elkind, *The Hurried Child*, x.
15. Ibid., xvii.
16. Ibid., 164.

of today do not allow this to happen. Our children, even before they reach the adolescent years, are stressed out. Because of the high divorce rate and increase of two-parent working scenarios, more and more children are assuming adult responsibilities at home. They experience emotional overload. Schools also stress children today beyond the typical issues associated with competition for grades. They are much more a host of theft and violence, and they tend to stereotype children and impose false expectancies on them. Elkind believes children are increasingly taught in environments that impede effective learning.[17] He suggests that contemporary media hurries children in one of two different ways: "they may give children too much information too fast, or they may give young people information that is too complex or abstract for children to understand. The first kind of hurrying produces the stress of information overload; the second produces the stress of emotional overload."[18]

If the entire faith community, adults and youth alike, regularly engaged in lament it would challenge them to slow down. Old Testament scholar Walter Brueggemann suggests, " . . . the lament-complaint, perhaps Israel's most characteristic and vigorous mode of faith, introduces us to a 'spirituality of protest.' That is, Israel boldly recognizes that all is not right in the world."[19] Elkind proclaims that not all is right with this fast-paced American society. Perhaps we need more people of faith protesting this reality that hurts our children and youth. Lament offers an avenue to faithfully express our protest to God and to each other. Furthermore, the lament found in Lamentations challenges people of faith to become compassionate advocates on behalf of the vulnerable and those who suffer. Perhaps our faith community needs to take up this call as we recognize the vulnerability of our children and youth.[20]

17. Ibid., 176.

18. Ibid., 181.

19. Brueggemann, "Foreword," xii.

20. O'Conner, *Lamentations and the Tears of the World*, 35–41.

Abandoned Youth

Chap Clark, author of *Hurt 2.0: Inside the World of Today's Teenagers*, argues that the defining issue for contemporary adolescents, particularly midadolescents, is abandonment. Building off the work of David Elkind, Clark uses the term "abandonment" rather than "hurry."[21] The adult world has systemically abandoned the youth of this generation from both external and internal systems.

Externally, the adult-driven institutions, including schools and churches, are primarily concerned with adult agendas, needs, and dreams.[22] In recent decades, our society has moved from "being a relatively stable and cohesive adult community intent on caring for the needs of the young to a free-for-all of independent and fragmented adults seeking their own survival . . . deepening a hole of systemic rejection. This rejection, or abandonment, of adolescents is the root of the fragmentation and calloused distancing that are the hallmarks of the adolescent culture."[23]

Internally, adolescents have suffered from the loss of safe relationships and intimate settings, primarily due to the re-definement of "family" in our culture.[24] There has been a shift in the past three decades from when the definition of family was accepted to be "two or more persons related by birth, marriage or adoption who reside in the same household to the current definition of a free-flowing, organic 'commitment' between people who love each other."[25] A second shift within families is the increased divorce rate over the past several decades. As previously stated, "We moved from a culture with a divorce rate that affected 2 percent of the married population in 1940 (264,000) to a society in which 43 percent of first-time marriages end in separation or divorce within fifteen years of marriage, as of 2002. Recent statistics show that in

21. Clark, *Hurt 2.0*, 27.

22. Ibid., 30.

23. Ibid., 15.

24. Ibid., 34–35.

25. Ibid., 16.

2008, 67 percent of children ages zero to seventeen lived with two married parents, down from 77 percent in 1980."[26]

For adolescents who yearn for stability and safety, societal choices regarding divorce, adult sexuality, and experimentation of living together does impact them. Clark advocates, "We are a culture that has forgotten how to be together. We have lost the ability to spend unstructured down time. Rather than being with children in creative activities at home or setting them free to enjoy semisupervised activities such as 'play,' we as a culture have looked to outside organizations and structured agendas to fill their time and dictate their lives."[27]

Since youth are abandoned by the adult institutions in their lives, they are forced to deal with pain and fear on their own. They have created a "world beneath," which is the adolescent response to systemic abandonment, a unique and defended social system. This world exists because they believe they have no choice and are searching for a relationally focused safe home to band together. While it is clear that young people are resilient, traumatic events related to systemic abandonment are permanent reminders of this rejection, which can cause significant psychological suffering years later.[28] However, in spite of all this, Clark still suggests that youth want adults and desire genuine, authentic relationships with them even though he ultimately found a greater chasm between adults and youth than he anticipated.

Of all the biblical genres, lament offers youth a chance to name those areas where they feel abandoned, even if it is seemingly from God. Perhaps this is best modeled by Jesus in his "My God, my God . . . " cry on the cross. Lament will empower young people to honestly express their frustrations, hopelessness, and pain associated with adults not being there for them or forcing their adult agendas onto them. However, lament also invites them to consider the fidelity of God to God's people, even when there are times of God's seeming absence. Practices of lament enable adolescents to

26. Ibid., 16.
27. Ibid., 31.
28. Ibid., 48.

be honest with themselves, to God, and to their faith community about their experiences of abandonment.

Adolescent Developmental Understandings

Much of adolescent developmental studies is based on the work of Erik Erikson who formulated his theories in the mid-twentieth century. His "eight stages of man" are often thought of and taught in blocks like a series of boxcars, one attached to the next as development proceeds. "In such a 'boxcar' conceptualization, events that are disruptive to development (whether conceived of as outer or inner events or conflicts) must be understood as impeding forward movement."[29] These disruptive events are seen as either stopping development, slowing it down, or derailing it until such a time exists when the boxcar of development is put back on the proper track again through counseling or other healing measures.

Pamela Cooper-White, a professor of pastoral theology and care and counseling, contends, "There is one serious conceptual problem with this boxcar formulation, however: biological maturation proceeds, even if development is damaged. In that process of maturation—simply 'growing up'—physical, cognitive, and affective growth does continue, although it might be compromised in some areas, even very prominent areas."[30] For example, not all victims of abuse respond to their childhood trauma in the same manner. Some engage in acts of "teenage rebellion," while others become all-A students or star athletes by taking refuge in their excellence. Some parts of the personality might seem stunted or missing or suffering great pain, but other parts grow according to normal expectations enabling people to overlook the deep, hidden pain.

I suggest two other helpful models of development to place alongside Erikson's boxcar approach. The first is Anna Freud's concept of "developmental lines." She proposed that "there is not a single line of development but rather a number of lines running

---

29. Cooper-White, "Opening the Eyes," 90.

30. Ibid., 90.

more or less parallel from infancy and on into adulthood . . . trauma might affect some but not all aspects of development, accounting for the appearance of competence and even precocity in many abused children . . . If certain experiences are too terrible to be assimilated, they may become encapsulated or frozen on certain developmental lines, while other aspects of development are freed to proceed in relative coordination with maturation."[31] This model reminds us as adult spiritual caregivers that there are multiple areas of growth within the same person and not everyone matures holistically. For example, someone who displays an overdeveloped capacity or strength in one area of life may be underdeveloped in areas of fragility, vulnerability, or fear.

A second model, proposed by Cooper-White, is that of the concentric rings of a tree trunk. Experiences during the earliest child development eras are encircled within or beneath later ones. Developmental achievements are layered together with the life experiences, joys, and crises of a particular time in life. "New growth forms around the old, rather than replacing it. Nothing is left behind. Trauma in this model might then be seen as having a number of manifestations, from being encapsulated like a nodule that later layers of growth cover but leave intact, to spreading throughout a particular layer of the trunk, rendering the whole tree more vulnerable to the impact of disease, cold, and storms . . . Helping in this model would not be conceptualized so much as getting something back on track, as going deeper, toward the core of the organism to tend enclosed wounds in need of healing and regeneration."[32]

Effects of trauma on development

I believe that increases in teenage suicide, eating disorders, and other mental health issues are signs of their inability to cope with the various crises, traumas, and losses that young people live with.

31. Ibid., 92.
32. Ibid., 92–93.

The accumulated levels of change and expectations are taking their toll on American adolescents!

Pain and loss are experienced in childhood, long before the adolescent years, and often times become repressed only to act itself out later in life. For example, in cases of child abuse, the repression of that brutality may eventually drive people to destroy their lives and the lives of others. Psychologist Alice Miller states, "In an unconscious thirst for revenge, they may engage in acts of violence, burning homes and businesses and physically attacking other people, using this destruction to hide the truth from themselves and avoid feeling the despair of the tormented child they once were."[33] A well known fact about many perpetrators of child abuse is that they were abused as children. Repressed pain may also reveal itself more privately. A woman sexually exploited as a child and who has denied this reality in later years in order not to feel the pain is "perpetually fleeing her past with the help of men, alcohol, drugs, or achievement. She needs a constant thrill to keep boredom at bay . . . she will continue in her flight unless she learns that the awareness of old feelings is not deadly but liberating."[34] The past may very well dictate the actions of the present.

Unfortunately, such abuse is more common in our society than we may realize or accept. Some studies suggest that up to 40 percent of females[35] and nearly 10 percent of males[36] under the age of eighteen have been sexually abused or assaulted. Other studies suggest that each year at least 10 percent of young people report being sexually abused by their parents, and another 10 percent report being physically abused by parents. However, these numbers are considered gross underestimates of the actual situation.[37] Related to abuse is the use of alcohol and drugs. Even back in 1999 "[a]mong confirmed cases of child abuse and neglect, about forty percent involve alcohol and other drugs. Almost 14 million

---

33. Miller, *The Drama of the Gifted Child*, 2.

34. Ibid., 3.

35. Rowatt, *Adolescents in Crisis*, 99.

36. Cooper-White, "Opening the Eyes," 88.

37. Parrott, *Helping the Struggling Adolescent*, 71.

adult Americans abuse alcohol and 12 million use illicit drugs. It is estimated that 9 to 10 million children and teens live in homes affected by substance-abusing parents."[38] Today, the Centers for Disease Control and Prevention authorities state, "Alcohol and other drug use among our nation's youth remains a major public health problem. Substance use and abuse can increase the risk for injuries, violence, HIV infection, and other diseases."[39]

Obviously not all victims of abuse act out in the same way, but one question for adolescent spiritual caregivers to consider is this: when will any type of behavior manifest itself—before, during, or after adolescence? Will such actions be perceived by the family or faith leader as "teenage rebellion"? Perhaps church leaders will challenge these young people to simply "get right with the Lord" and overlook the painful roots of these behaviors. An adolescent who is rebuked for such behavior may further internalize this and believe everything is their fault. This may lead to further destructive choices or denial of their childhood or present realities. These wounds cannot truly heal without the work of intentional mourning and grief.

Jaco Hamman, associate professor of religion, psychology, and culture, suggests that *grief* "is the normal emotional, spiritual, physical, and relational reaction to the experience of loss and change,"[40] whereas *mourning* "is the intentional process of letting go of relationships, dreams, and visions as [you] live into a new identity after the experience of loss and change."[41] Hamman contends that the work of mourning is a creative response to loss. A church leader should facilitate the work of mourning. Lament is an intentional process of assisting young people to appropriately relinquish and mourn their identified losses in ways that may lead to healing and restoration rather than destructive behaviors. However, as adult spiritual caregivers come into contact with adolescent

38. Weaver et al., *Counseling Troubled Teens and Their Families*, 76.

39. Centers for Disease Control and Prevention, "Alcohol and Other Drug Use," lines 2–4.

40. Hamman, *When Steeples Cry*, 12.

41. Ibid., 13.

trauma, they should make necessary referrals to their pastor or other trained caregivers for counseling or other appropriate means of help. Engaging biblical lament is one way for young people to grieve and mourn their losses, but it dare not be viewed as "the only way" of response for effects of trauma on development.

Exception or Normalcy?

Such trauma may seem to be the exception and so most programmed youth ministry efforts neglect such realities. But consider the following: "Fifty percent of today's youth may experience a major crisis before reaching the age of eighteen. They will be hospitalized, appear in court, have major potential conflicts, be crippled in an accident, attempt suicide, abuse alcohol, drop out of school, get pregnant, contract a sexually transmitted disease, be arrested, be raped, pay for or have an abortion, witness an act of violence, or experience something else of this magnitude," writes adolescent counselor G. Wade Rowatt.[42] Yet the word "crisis" has also been used by developmental psychologist Erik Erikson and others to describe the struggles of adolescent development, in terms of *identity crisis*. The word "crisis" might conjure up the notion that such experiences are out-of-the-ordinary. However, "for developmentalists, a crisis is a turning point, the result of a struggle or threat to one's emotional security or physical danger"[43] and can result in opportunity for growth and change, or danger and destruction.

Rowatt's description of major crisis and that of identity crisis in adolescence can be considered two types of crises. The former, even though they seem to be out-of-the-ordinary accompanied by significant change and loss, are common among our adolescents today. Rowatt identifies these as disruptive or emergency crises, and the latter as developmental crises.[44] Developmental crises are

---

42. Rowatt, *Adolescents in Crisis*, 3.

43. Atkinson, *Ministry with Youth in Crisis*, 4.

44. Rowatt, *Adolescents in Crisis*, 25, 31, 38.

those expected issues that are part of growing up, such as gaining independence from parents, dating, developing peer relationships, and embracing personal identity. Even though disruptive crises may seem to illicit more pain and loss due to the unexpected nature of the trauma, developmental crises can also yield much accumulated grief if they go unattended.

With these two views of crises in mind, I do not wish to perpetuate a "storm and stress" view of adolescence that suggests the dark days and struggles will be over once they reach adulthood.[45] The losses and changes they endure are very real and should not be treated lightly. Similar issues of loss and change not only precede adolescence, but accompany them throughout adulthood. Such disruptive crises as death of loved ones and effects of divorce and abuse occur throughout life. Having reviewed some of the major, broad issues related to adolescent development, I now wish to explore some particularities among the various sub-stages of adolescence.

Preadolescence

As noted earlier, David Elkind suggests that adults "hurry" children to grow up. These preadolescent children act like and copy teenagers even though they have not yet begun puberty. Their dress and yearning for certain social freedoms demonstrate their desire to be considered teenagers, yet most lack the ability to cope with such adolescent pressures. Nevertheless, they are pushed and may push themselves intellectually, emotionally, and socially to grow up faster than they are ready. "Their biggest need is for more structure and adult involvement in their lives. They need the reassurance that grown-ups still care for them. Too much freedom is read as not showing an interest in them."[46]

45. Robbins, *This Way to Youth Ministry*, 176.
46. Rowatt, *Adolescents in Crisis*, 21.

Early Adolescence

Early adolescence begins with puberty. This is a time of rapid physical change and relationship adjustments that may feel like an emotional roller coaster. Because of the many developmental crises and changes they experience, they need avenues of success in their social encounters, physical activities, and intellectual endeavors. They also need "permission to discuss these changes and find support for the persons they are becoming. They need forgiveness for awkward mistakes and impulsive outbursts in the family system."[47] It is also important to recognize that in these early teen years they still reason in fairly defined categories of right and wrong, even though they are now more self-conscious and their thought processes are beginning to change.[48]

Disruptive crises of this age group may include the divorce of their parents, the death of a parent, a forced move to a new school, or an accident to themselves. "In such times, early adolescents especially need information about the crisis, a sustaining environment characterized by hope, and avenues of forgiveness for real or imaginary guilt. Younger teens need parents, teachers, ministers, and counselors who offer a supportive relationship that encourages the discussion of uncomfortable questions . . . They need permission to speak of previously taboo topics."[49]

Engaging practices of biblical lament can offer early adolescents permission to acknowledge and express their emotions. For these young people, they may internalize their painful feelings or respond to them with an over-abundance of guilt and shame. Lament lets them know that such feelings are normal, even if their anger is directed at God. Learning the broader stories surrounding the laments will help them know that others in the faith have suffered similar griefs, and God accepted their prayers. It will also be important that adult spiritual caregivers engage in practices of biblical lament themselves. This modeling also grants permission

---

47. Ibid., 25.

48. Dunn, *Shaping the Spiritual Life of Students*, 174.

49. Rowatt, *Adolescents in Crisis*, 25.

for these young people to vent their inner feelings, questions, frustrations, and confusions. Though articulating themselves in such ways may be challenging for some early adolescents, such practices will begin to establish a foundation for dealing with loss and grief.

In the study I described in chapter 3, it was quite clear that this age group simply appreciated the opportunity to express their emotions to God. They were quite comfortable with this way of engaging biblical lament even though this was a new experience for many of them. Their expressions of lament tended to involve the more concrete, everyday aspects of life such as school, friendships, and family.

Middle Adolescence

Middle adolescence is a time of expansion, independence, and experimentation. Continued physiological changes, independent thinking, and the questioning of authority while venturing into new peer relationships characterize this sub-stage. In fact, peer socialization will often dominate the lives of middle adolescents as they build deeper relationships with them and seemingly less so than with their parents. However, at their best, these peer groups do not supplant parents, but rather "they supplement them by providing a relational bridge for safely learning how to become independent."[50] Middle adolescents are able to think in new ways. They take the perspective of others' views of them into account and assume that everyone around them is concerned about them. In other words, they become more self-conscious, self-centered, and self-absorbed, and often think: "I am not who I think I am, I am not who you think I am, I am who I think you think I am."[51] Even though young people are now able to better engage in abstract thinking, it has been observed that "'midadolescents' ability

50. Dunn, *Shaping the Spiritual Life of Students*, 190.
51. Dunn, *Shaping the Spiritual Life of Students*, 192.

to engage in abstract thought is limited to the immediate context of a discussion."[52]

Though there continue to be many changes and new opportunities for these young people, developmental crises focus around the experiences of driving, dating, and distancing.[53] Auto accidents are the number one killer of youth and so youth may need to better accept responsibility for and learn the necessary driving skills. Dating is another area that may bring about new levels of joy, excitement, and affirmation, but it can also create new depths of grief, rejection, and pain. Distance from parents is understood in terms of freedom. "Parents who are too strict urge their strong children toward rebellion . . . However, parents who provide few stable values and resist limit setting push teens into experimenting. Adolescents with good ego strength will be able to set limits for themselves, but those with weaker ego strength may fall off either end of a continuum. Some will become so anxious and frightened by freedom that they begin to deteriorate emotionally, whereas others will become so enamored of freedom that they act out behaviorally."[54]

Disruptive crises for middle adolescents often relate to family, substance abuse, school, sex, depression and illnesses. "If the family system deteriorates, middle adolescents will frequently blame themselves and grieve deeply. Grief over the end of their parents' marriage and unbearable self-blame, for example, may lead to acting out sexually, to attempting to escape into alcohol and drug abuse."[55] It is estimated that between 30 to 75 percent of these young people are sexually active, thereby increasing the number of crises related to pregnancy, sexually transmitted diseases, emotional rejection, abuse, and rape; date rape accounts for most cases of rape.[56] Unfortunately, the instances of physical and sexual abuse

---

52. Clark, *Hurt 2.0*, 19.
53. Rowatt, *Adolescents in Crisis*, 30.
54. Ibid., 30.
55. Ibid., 31.
56. Ibid., 27.

increases during middle adolescence.[57] "In this time of expansion and exploration, middle adolescents need time and space to reflect and learn from their [disruptive] crises. They need some system of forgiveness for their own mistakes and also an experience of grace that accepts their attempts to discover themselves. Although they must admit their mistakes, they need reassurance that they did not cause all their problems."[58] Above all, even though experimentation may lead to accidents and illnesses, these young people need a place to talk about major concerns.

Engaging practices of lament with middle adolescents offers them space for reflection and a practical, tangible way to do it. It will strengthen their skills needed for constructive reflection. Lament offers grace to young people by letting them know that a wide array of emotions is normal and that others have experienced similar struggles. But perhaps more importantly, grace is experienced in the movement of the plea to the praise. Structurally, biblical lament will often end in authentic praise because of some experience or encounter with God. In some ways, one could view the intense emotions surrounding a particular crisis event as part of a "liminal experience," hanging between the "what was" and the "what will be." Lament enables the questions, confusions, doubts, and angers of liminality to be voiced to God and God's people. And, God receives these prayers of anguish. By engaging practices of lament, it may curb the tendency of midadolescents to blame themselves of all the troubles they experience, particularly in cases of parental divorce that is of no fault to the teenager.

The overwhelming majority of the youth in this age group who participated in the project described in chapter 3 appreciated the opportunity to vent and express their honest emotions to God. They valued knowing that God wanted them to be true in their words and that God yearned for such an authentic, intimate relationship with them. A significant number of them believed that this way of praying actually helped their relationship with God and with the church. Compared to the early adolescents, their prayers

57. Ibid., 30.
58. Ibid., 32.

of lament tended to be more abstract in nature and touched on themes of personal struggles with sin, human greed, loneliness, human and family suffering, abandonment, and struggles with various types of relationships.

Late Adolescence

Late adolescence is less tied to a chronology of events compared to that of early and middle. It is a shift from experimentation to a mode of refinement and consolidation as late adolescents begin to focus on jobs, education, and life partnerships. However, not all middle adolescents become mature enough to embrace typical late adolescent issues, and so they become stagnated in middle adolescence. "Although some young people never stop experimenting . . . [it] is time to refine the data gathered through their experimentation and to consolidate those data into a view of self, family, peers, society, sacredness, and the future. For persons not able to move into late adolescence, the experimentation stage may continue into the twenties and beyond . . . For some persons, experimentation in delayed adolescence becomes a life-style, uncritically adopted, until a midlife crisis forces the refinement and consolidation task upon them."[59]

Developmental crises common in late adolescence focus on the three major tasks of developing an identity, deciding on vocation, and forming intimate relationships with a potential life partner.[60] For one of the first times in their lives, these late adolescent emerging adults are trying on adult roles as they seek to solidify an identity. A growing capacity for self-awareness prompts a desire to connect more intimately with people, particularly as they seriously consider marriage.[61] They seek to compose a coherent worldview as they labor to synthesize past beliefs of their childhood and

---

59. Ibid., 33.

60. Ibid., 37.

61. Dunn, *Shaping the Spiritual Life of Students*, 210.

teenage years, with their present learning and new experiences.[62] It is important to remember that as late adolescents complete high school, undergraduate and graduate studies, they will no longer have the educational system to serve as an undergirding framework for their lives. This may be a significant shock to them.

Disruptive (emergency) crises can erupt when developmental needs go unfulfilled. The three major areas involve pregnancy, legal issues, and substance abuse. As stated previously, the rate of adolescent suicide has significantly increased over the past few decades. Nearly twenty years ago, young women attempted suicide four times more frequently than did males, but the male to female ratio of completed suicides was four to one.[63] And, Caucasian males over the age of sixteen were at the greatest risk since about three out of four young adult suicides are among this group of young people.[64] Today, authorities at the Center for Disease Control and Prevention state, "A nationwide survey of youth in grades 9–12 in public and private schools in the United States (U.S.) found that 16% of students reported seriously considering suicide, 13% reported creating a plan, and 8% reporting trying to take their own life in the 12 months preceding the survey. Each year, approximately 157,000 youth between the ages of 10 and 24 receive medical care for self-inflicted injuries at Emergency Departments across the U.S . . . .Boys are more likely than girls to die from suicide. Of the reported suicides in the 10 to 24 age group, 81% of the deaths were males and 19% were females. Girls, however, are more likely to report attempting suicide than boys."[65] Though there are multiple reasons and risk factors for adolescent suicide including family problems, personal loss, social isolation, and substance abuse, the most common denominator of suicide risk for adolescents is depression.[66]

62. Ibid., 217.

63. Weaver et al., *Counseling Troubled Teens and Their Families*, 172.

64. Ibid., 174.

65. Centers for Disease Control and Prevention, "Suicide Prevention: Youth Suicide," lines 9–13, 15–18.

66. Weaver et al., *Counseling Troubled Teens and Their Families*, 247;

For adult spiritual caregivers, perhaps one of the best gifts they can offer to these young adults is a safe environment to ask fearful questions and guide them into critical reflection. "Critical reflection is the process of examining the why behind the what of one's life. Late adolescence should be considered the prime time for the formation of critical reflection skills and habits."[67] In a similar vein, mentoring young adults is also key to their successful navigation through the developmental and disruptive crises they experience. "[G]ood mentors play a vital role in stewarding the promise of a worthy future. As emerging adults are beginning to think critically about self and world, mentors provide crucial forms of recognition, support, and challenge."[68]

Practices of biblical lament offer a place of grace and reflection in the midst of the many transitions, changes, and losses experienced by late adolescents. Adult mentors can guide these young people through the engagement of biblical lament as they listen to their profound questions and joys of life. If a group of young adults regularly practice lament with each other, it would foster a safe environment for vulnerabilities to be shared with one another. Authors of biblical lament may serve as "mentoring figures" to them even if they are no longer alive or have never met them.

The post-high school group of people who participated in the project described in chapter 3 overwhelmingly enjoyed the space and structure to vent their problems and express their feelings to God. Some of them even recalled some painful memories and frustrations they thought had been resolved, but were not. Common themes of their prayers centered around yearning for a deeper intimacy with God and clarity in vocational direction. As with the other two age groups, most of them believed that their family and friends would enjoy engaging biblical lament in some fashion.

Rowatt, *Adolescents in Crisis*, 147.

67. Dunn, *Shaping the Spiritual Life of Students*, 222.

68. Daloz Parks, *Big Questions, Worthy Dreams*, 165.

Key Pastoral Care Concepts

Now that I have reviewed some of the specific characteristics associated with early, middle, and late adolescence and have suggested some ways that biblical lament may serve as a resource for young people in their journey, I will now offer some key pastoral care concepts and ideas to be kept in mind as adult spiritual caregivers walk with all young people.

Resilience

Young people are resilient beings. Resilience suggests that after being stretched or bent, there is a return to an original shape.[69] It describes the ability to recover from a significant suffering or traumatic event, but at the same time, it requires a set of characteristics that foster successful healing and growth in the face of potential harm and high risk. Resiliency begins with a person's determination to survive and optimism about doing well, but it is also reinforced by achievement.[70] There are other significant external factors that foster a sense of resiliency: a strong family support system; an ability to find other sources of help and support, particularly an important person outside the family system; being well liked by friends and peers; finding a safe sanctuary away from the chaotic situation; participating in extracurricular activities; and help from a church group or minister.

However, we must also be careful not to simply dismiss the seriousness of developmental and disruptive crises young people face and expect resiliency to carry them through. Afterall, if this were the case then there would be no reason for an escalation in the rate of teenage suicides. Chap Clark warns us, "While it is fairly clear that adolescents are resilient, traumatic events are permanent reminders of abandonment that can cause significant psychological suffering many years down the road. Being resilient to trauma is similar to 'getting over' the loss of an arm. The consequences of

69. Borgman, *Hear My Story*, 153.

70. Ibid., 155.

a ripped-apart family system remain a constant source of broken-ness throughout one's life."[71]

Nevertheless, walking with young people in the midst of their loss fosters a sense of resilience not only for them as individuals, but also for the resilience of the family, faith community, and other support groups. Young people cannot go at it alone, but adult spiritual caregivers should not feel that it is solely up to them to lead youth through the despairs of life. Ultimately, we need each other. We in the faith community need the resources and support of what all the local community has to offer. In this way, resilience stems from a shared responsibility "when they result in practices that contribute to the resilience of children [and adolescents] and those who care for them, the kind of resilience that continues to share responsibility despite overwhelming odds, gains, and disappointments, a resilience that is tenacious because it arises from God's grace."[72]

Religious communities can offer crucial resources to help with the emotional needs of youth and their families. However, for church communities to do this they will need to be prepared to walk with the challenges of today and know the resources at their own disposal, particularly those in the local community. Dean Borgman points out that there still remains a question as to why some people are more resilient than others and that we dare not deny the power of God's grace in the midst of deep suffering.[73] As adult spiritual caregivers it will be important for us to find and cre-ate opportunities for grace to abound. This could include certain cleansing ceremonies and healing rituals.[74]

Engaging biblical lament has a role to play in the degree to which adolescent youth will display increased levels of resiliency. Lament offers the individual a way of authentically crying out to God. They may compose their own or read those found in Psalms, Lamentations, or by other writers such as Ann Weems, who wrote

71. Clark, *Hurt 2.0*, 48.
72. Couture, *Seeing Children, Seeing God*, 16.
73. Borgman, *Hear My Story*, 153.
74. Ibid., 154.

a collection of laments following the death of her son in a book titled *Psalms of Lament*. Adult spiritual caregivers can also conduct services or worship experiences for their entire adolescent group that center around lament. This too creates a space for God's grace to intervene in the midst of the gathered group. It gives young people permission and structure to cry out to God, particularly if they are uncomfortable doing so individually. But more importantly, a youth group that regularly engages in corporate practices of lament can become that safe, supportive sanctuary away from the chaotic or traumatic situation in life. Finally, it is suggested that Lamentations is an expression and tribute to a resilient community who faced cataclysmic loss.[75] Learning more of this story may help the resiliency factor for both individuals and groups.

Eschatological Hope

As we walk with young people, both individually and collectively, it will be important that we instill a sense of hope. In *Counseling Troubled Youth*, Robert Dykstra suggests an eschatological theology of hope is key to counseling youth who are in despair. Because of the increased rates of teenage suicide, homicide, eating disorders, drugs and alcohol, and sexual abuse, as well as the increased reality of one-parent households and academic pressures, he believes there is a widespread loss of hope and faith.[76] Other symptoms of this despair include apathy, shame and guilt, preoccupation with violence and death, blurring of self and others, dislocation of rootedness and tradition, and various compulsive "hungers."[77] In other words, the growing and diverse cultural ills of our society nurture youth in such a way that harms their holistic development of adolescent selves. Obviously, this affects who they become as adults.

As a foundation for walking with young people in ways that lead to restored wholeness, Dykstra emphasizes the doctrine of Christian hope that reminds the reader of Jesus' suffering and

75. Dobbs-Allsopp, *Lamentations*, 2.

76. Dykstra, *Counseling Troubled Youth*, 1.

77. Ibid., 2.

resurrection.[78] The neglect of a crucified Jesus results in a neglect of human need and suffering to maintain the status quo. Even though a doctrine of hope is grounded in the realities of our past and present, human identity is more tied to the future. Dykstra notes two understandings of the future: *futurum* and *adventus*. The former is the "projecting forward in time what we already know in the present and that which will likely 'will be,'" whereas the latter refers to "the advent or adventure of something new, some event that could in no way develop out of past or present, the foundation of Christian hope . . . God's essential nature is in God's *coming*, not in God's *becoming*." [79] For Dykstra, the pastoral caregiver is to walk with youth while the *futurum* is happening, but also to nurture them toward the anticipation of the *adventus* and then be prepared to help them unfold this experience.

The eschatological self is "already, but not yet." Cultivating the eschatological self is a theological way of expressing the self's experience of newness, surprise, and hope.[80] Therefore, one's self is not solely determined by the past. Furthermore, the eschatological self is not utopian or escapist, but holds in agonizing tension the past, present, and future. It intentionally engages our current and past realities; it is the cross and resurrection together.[81]

Biblical lament holds in tension that of painful reality and authentic praise. Lament will empower young people to resist tendencies to flee reality or deny their emotions. Instead, it demands honesty and introspective truthfulness. Naming their pain and suffering may begin their healing process, and open adolescents up to other realities or that of the *adventus*. Furthermore, lament assures young people that God is listening to them and receiving all of their prayers, especially in the midst of the ups and downs of life.

78. Ibid., 6.
79. Ibid., 14.
80. Ibid., 17.
81. Ibid., 89.

Conclusion

In his book *Boy's Passage, Man's Journey*, Brian Molitor suggests that lifelong mentoring, intentional blessings, and rites of passage are needed to help boys become mature Christian men. As a father, Molitor is writing this book to other fathers and men of faith. He also acknowledges that many of the principles in this book can be applied to girls and women as well. This book is a response to the current woes and struggles of our society. Some aspects of this book can be helpful to all adult spiritual caregivers. In particular, I want to highlight his final chapter, "Healing a Father's Heart."

He suggests that every man has been wounded and his heart broken at some point in his life. Those wounds can limit the effectiveness of a father to adequately mentor and bless their sons and daughters. "Left to fester, these wounds caused by rejection, abuse, abandonment, and fear cloud our judgment about who we are and why we are here. They also cause us to withdraw, lash out, criticize, and even reject the precious young ones God has given us to protect. When we acknowledge our pain and allow God to heal us, then the hearts that we turn toward our children will be pure, whole, and full of love for them. This will take courage to accomplish."[82]

For all adult spiritual caregivers, whether they are parents, pastors, or youthworkers, we all bear past wounds and hurts. We continue to encounter painful experiences in life. The ability for us to properly walk with young people in the midst of their own suffering, demands that we too engage our own brokenness. One way for us to address our own pains is to engage in biblical lament ourselves. To authentically lead youth in practices and exercises of lament, we will have needed to face and engage those issues that call us to cry out to God. As we do, God's grace may affect us in ways that lead to healing. If so, then these stories should also be told to adolescents as a way of not only modeling faith to them, but more importantly as a visible testimony. Molitor warns that "if we wait until we are completely whole, then we lose the opportunity to lead countless young people . . . "[83]

82. Molitor, *Boy's Passage, Man's Journey*, 205–206.

83. Molitor, *Boy's Passage, Man's Journey*, 208.

5

The Role of Biblical Lament in Faith Formation of Adolescents

Why must this pain be afflicted on me?

Why does the sorrow never end?

Why do you not reveal the needed light in my life of darkness?

You promise to show me a light.

You have been there for me in my struggles.

You hear me and cry with me through the long weary nights. I can always trust in you.

You shall never forsake me.

You are right beside me always and forever.

You are the beginning and the end.

—TEENAGER

Alone . . .

all alone . . .

no one to share the isolation with

no one to lift me up and know my sadness.

God, you are here, you hold me and cuddle me close

You see deeply into me . . . feel my pain . . .

You alone can wash away the sadness, the bleak and cold from within me.

I praise you God for your presence.

You alone are always near

Willing to withstand the cold and bring warmth.

—TEENAGER

DAVID WHITE, IN *PRACTICING Discernment with Youth: A Transformative Youth Ministry Approach*, argues that youth today are passive consumers compared to pre-Industrialized youth. The American educational system constantly seeks to prepare them for the future, rather than reflectively engage them in the present; delaying their entrance into adulthood. The media market overwhelms young people by feeding off their youthful energies. This same market demands their compliance and passivity; detaching and numbing them to the material conditions around them.[1] Even our churches domesticate their prophetic voices and marginalize them from the larger faith community; distorting and rendering them apathetic, low in self-esteem, unstable in identity, and prone to violence or alienation.[2]

Furthermore, White contends that today's popular youth ministry efforts leave our young people ill equipped for lifelong discipleship.[3] In the past several decades, youth ministry had been left to independent commercial enterprises that failed to

1. White, *Practicing Discernment with Youth*, 17–19.
2. Ibid., 39.
3. Ibid., 5.

recognize one's own denomination, theology, ethnicity, and class, nor able to critique the social roles of young people. Discipleship, according to White, requires attentiveness to the holy, prophetic social critique, justice-seeking action, compassionate responses to all creation, and a commitment to transformative, mutual relationships that bring congruence to *imago dei* ("image of God").[4]

White describes the following as core tensions of youth ministry today: youth are distracted by the demands of success; youth are marginalized by the faith community; youth are detached from the material conditions of the community; it is difficult to engage youth in theological reflection; and there is much isolation, burnout, and turnover of youth ministers.[5] For White, the future of youth ministry must include practices that equip young people and their congregations with skills for bringing the gospel into creative tension with questions and circumstances for our lives.[6]

What can we do as adult spiritual caregivers? How can we curb their focus on material success to include the real needs of the broken-hearted and impoverished around them? How can we better draw people into the larger faith community, both their immediate one and the historical one? How can we teach young people to engage in theological reflection and critique? If it is true that there is a high turnover rate of youth ministers, what can be done to nurture their own spiritual souls that yield a longer, more consistent walk with young people?

I suggest that engaging biblical lament can be one of those practices that will equip young people for lifelong discipleship. It will challenge them to reflect on the personal losses they have experienced, as well as the suffering of other people around them and in the world. The practice of lament is a theological enterprise that demands they consider God's role in this world, as well as their own. Doing so will engage them with their world and faith community, rather than passively sit on the sidelines. As adult spiritual caregivers lead young people in the practice of biblical

4. Ibid., vii.

5. Ibid., 42–57.

6. Ibid., 60.

lament, they too will mature in their own faith while teaching youth necessary skills that brings the gospel into creative tension with the world around them.

In this chapter I will overview the cultural landscape of adolescents by reviewing the findings from the National Study of Youth and Religion and further explore the distortions of an overly-consumeristic culture. Then I will highlight key adolescent faith development issues, giving attention to their general longings as well as specific considerations of early, middle, and late adolescence. Throughout this chapter I will propose ways to engage practices of biblical lament that will appropriately respond to the challenges raised from our culture and within the adolescent journey.

Cultural Landscape

Religious and Spiritual Lives of Adolescents

The National Study of Youth and Religion (NSYR), a comprehensive sociological project conducted at the University of North Carolina from 2001-2015 and led by principal investigator Dr. Christian Smith, published the first phase of their findings in the book *Soul Searching: The Religious and Spiritual Lives of American Teenagers.* "The purpose of the NSYR is to research the shape and influence of religion and spirituality in the lives of American youth; to identify effective practices in the religious, moral, and social formation of the lives of youth; to describe the extent and perceived effectiveness of the programs and opportunities that religious communities are offering to their youth; and to foster an informed national discussion about the influence of religion in youth's lives, in order to encourage sustained reflection about and rethinking of our cultural and institutional practices with regard to youth and religion."[7] I believe the conclusions in this book offer both challenge and hope.

First, the researchers discovered that religion is a significant presence in the lives of many U.S. teens today. In fact, most

7. National Study of Youth and Religion, "Research Purpose," lines 1–5.

teenagers generally feel positive toward religion and the institutional church.[8] However, religion operates in a weak social structural position compared to other activities and organizations that lay claim to their time. Religion is simply not a priority for most youth. Furthermore, the spiritual and religious understanding among teens is very weak. For the most part, they are inarticulate about their faith beliefs.

As a response to these findings, Smith suggests that parents and faith communities not be shy about teaching teens and to work much harder on articulation of faith understandings. He notes, "We were astounded by the realization that for very many teens we interviewed, it seemed as if our interview was the first time any adult had ever asked them what they believed. By contrast, the same teens could be remarkably articulate about other subjects about which they had been drilled, such as drinking, drugs, STDs, and safe sex."[9] Fostering articulation means that we need to help teens practice talking about their faith by providing usable vocabularies, stories, and key messages of faith.

Engaging in biblical lament will help youth articulate their obscure feelings, emotions, frustrations, and questions. Reading and praying through biblical laments will begin to offer them a grammar and vocabulary of faith. Composing their own personal laments, either for themselves or on behalf of others, will connect their own developing life story with the ongoing "God story." If youth are able to intellectually talk about drugs, safe sex, and other rehearsed issues, then perhaps identifying the accompanying faith questions and struggles surrounding these issues can also help connect them with key concepts of faith.

A second key conclusion is that supply and demand matters to the spiritual lives of teenagers. The greater the availability of religiously grounded relationships, activities, programs, opportunities, and challenges for teens, the more likely they are to be religiously engaged and invested. In other words, "congregations [conferences, denominations] that prioritize youth ministry and support for

8. Smith, *Soul Searching*, 260.
9. Ibid., 267.

their parents, invest in trained and skilled youth group leaders, and make serious efforts to engage and teach adolescents seem much more likely to draw youth into their religious lives and to foster religious and spiritual maturity in their young members."[10]

This point, I believe, connects with a study undertaken by Carol Lytch where she focused on the religious lives of high school seniors.[11] Lytch noted previous research documenting the disappearance from churches and youth groups of church-going youth during their junior and senior years of high school; the dropout rate accelerates after graduation. She examined three churches from evangelical protestant, mainline protestant, and Catholic traditions that were putting extra effort into engaging their teens through the end of their high school years to find out what kept them involved.[12] Overall she found that teens were attracted to those churches because they offered them a sense of belonging, a sense of meaning, and opportunities to develop competence.[13] In other words, these churches provided their youth with many meaningful opportunities that met the "supply and demand" factor, but more importantly youth ministry was a high priority for these churches.

Churches that proactively engage young people in practices of lament will connect them to the ongoing faith story that goes back thousands of years between God and God's people. By authentically and transparently crying out to God in ways knowing that God will receive those prayers lets young people know that they belong to God and to the ongoing faith community of God's people. When young people see adults lead in and engage biblical lament themselves, this too will create a safe space for youth to know of their acceptance by these adults. Lament offers a sense of meaning because it demands that young people know God's acceptance of their prayers and that these prayers will be heard by God. These prayers mean something to God and have the power

10. Ibid., 261–262.

11. Lytch, *Choosing Church*, ix.

12. Ibid., 8.

13. Ibid., 25.

to cause God to act in ways that bring about righteousness and justice on earth, as right relationships are restored. As adult spiritual caregivers regularly provide worship times and spaces to engage in practices of biblical lament, young people will grow more competent and confident in this way.

Third, NSYR concluded that teenagers tend to espouse a religious outlook that is distinct and different from traditional faith commitments of most U.S. religious traditions. This can be described as Moralistic Therapeutic Deism, which is: "1. A God exists who created and orders the world and watches over human life. 2. God wants people to be good, nice, and fair to each other, as taught in the Bible and by most world religions. 3. The central goal of life is to be happy and to feel good about oneself. 4. God does not need to be particularly involved in one's life except when God is needed to resolve a problem. 5. Good people go to heaven when they die."[14]

Biblical lament challenges the ideology of Moralistic Therapeutic Deism. Though most laments end in some sort of praise to God and God's faithfulness, it does not always promise a "happy ending" to life in the ways of American notions of security and prosperity. Lament tells the story of people who suffered, but who called out to a God in whom they believed was consistently active in the world, through good times and bad. God was the generator of life and played an active role in all of life's expressions, not just when problems arose. Psalms of creation, praise, and thanksgiving and other biblical stories testify to God's active presence. A biblical worldview locates God at the center of all things, not humans. Yes, human beings are God's wonderful creation, but God did not revolve around humanity. Today, however, it seems that we have adopted an anthropocentric worldview where humanity is at the center of all things. MTD suggests that humans are "gods of the universe." As noted in chapter 2, lament psalms offer a language that acknowledges God as Sovereign, not Self. Dwelling in this language helps us inhabit a biblical, theocentric worldview. [15]

14. Smith, *Soul Searching*, 162–163.

15. Jinkins, *In the House of the Lord*, 5.

One suggestion by Smith to counter teens' strong inclination toward individualism is that adult spiritual caregivers should "challenge their often highly conventional styles of doing religion and to bring faith issues out of the background and into the foreground of their lives."[16] Because biblical lament has often been neglected by the church for so long and because it does away with the "niceties" of addressing God, it may serve as a new expression of faith for many youth. Biblical lament will bring forth stories of faith overlooked by the church and empower young people to bring all aspects of their lives into dialogue with God and their faith community. Practices of lament may challenge certain life and faith assumptions, thereby provoking questions of whether they should simply go along with the standard norm or to examine if there are more faithful ways to live out God's desires for humanity. Lament will either stir up or resonate with critical questions adolescents already have about life, faith, and God's role in them rather than assume God is not involved. Discovering expressions of faithful living, I believe, gets at the core of nurturing lifelong discipleship.

NSYR found that the single most important influence on the religious and spiritual lives of adolescents is their parents.[17] In fact, most American teenagers follow in their parents' footsteps when it comes to religion, and thereby teenage religiosity is extraordinarily conventional. The "youth culture" described in *Soul Searching* suggests that the beliefs and practices of youth are really a mirror image of their parents' beliefs and practices. Perhaps the generations really are not that different, even though it may appear so at times on the surface.

This point is also confirmed in Lytch's research as she notes that the religious nurture of parents in later teen years does matter and make a difference in the lives of teens.[18] She concludes, " . . . regular family church attendance appears to be the most significant of all factors contributing to teen religious loyalty . . . "[19] But

16. Smith, *Soul Searching*, 268.
17. Ibid., 261.
18. Lytch, *Choosing Church*, 141.
19. Ibid., 183.

she also noted that when parental church attendance patterns differed, teenage attendance usually mirrored that of the least active parent. "If they want their child to attend, they must be willing to attend themselves."[20]

For me this is a point of hope—youth are "getting it." They do pick up and embody what is modeled to them by their parents and other adults. Young people are not a "strange breed" with whom we need to dissect and study in order to fully understand and relate. They value adult relationships and learn from them. If we are able to be authentic and appropriately transparent with them about our lives and faith, then they will "get it." However, the challenge for adults is that we need to actively engage in spiritual practices that will nurture our own spiritual formation and growth.

Again, this is where I see lament playing a crucial role not only in the faith formation of young people, but in the life of the entire faith community. Practices of lament, to truly take root, will need to be engaged by parents, adult spiritual caregivers, and other adult leaders and people in the faith community. I believe it is critical that all pastoral and congregational leaders pave the way in engaging practices of biblical lament for the entire faith community. Participating in biblical lament will help to create a more faithful community who strives to follow God's call on their lives in this world. The hopeful and transformative power of lament lies in everyone's honesty with God when we remember those times in the past of how God had been faithful, which then may have led to a life of authentic praise of God. Hearing biblical laments and praying them ourselves will have a shaping and transformative impact on adolescents and adults alike.

The Power of a Consumeristic Culture

One of the challenges that adult spiritual caregivers face today is the discretionary time and money that our young people possess.[21]

---

20. Ibid., 177.
21. Dunn, *Shaping the Spiritual Life of Students*, 37.

Media and marketing take advantage of this as products and experiences are shown to young people over and over, calling out for their time, money, and loyalty. However, there is a symbiotic relationship between youth and the media of youth culture. As music and media companies learn what sells to young people when new artists are introduced, they will spend millions of dollars in marketing to target and sell to the tastes of these young people. In this way, youth also possess an influential power on these companies.

In our individualistic, self-centered American culture, "the culture assists individuals in making peace with whatever they choose as the path to personal fulfillment."[22] In this way our culture is therapeutic. Rather than confronting and challenging individual's beliefs, convictions, and commitments, popular culture simply gives the consumer what they want. Popular consumeristic culture shapes young people to ask, "How much more do I want?" rather than "Will this be good for my and my community's health, well-being, and faith?"

When our relatively old gadgets and toys do not satisfy our cravings, even though we may have purchased them a few months prior, we will need something that is faster, quicker to download, louder, more extravagant, flashier, and more compact with bigger memory. Forces in our culture appeal to our sensate mentality that "is interested only in those things, usually the material in nature, that appeal to or affect our senses. It seeks the imposing, the impressive, the voluptuous; it encourages self-indulgence."[23] Before long, such a sensate worldview will have adolescents gauge the value of their lives by the level of sensory payoff.[24] We will have become pleasure pragmatists and possess an "If it feels good, do it" attitude. This does not encourage us to consider how we or others will be affected.

Practices of biblical lament will challenge young people to slow down and consider the cries of this world, including the injustices that their friends and neighbors may be experiencing.

22. Ibid., 37.
23. Ibid., 39.
24. Ibid., 40.

Lament will help young people see the world through the eyes of the marginalized since so many of these biblical authors experienced hardship in ways that placed them outside the dominant power structure. Lament verbalized the reality of people feeling marginalized even by God. As young people learn more about the tensions of those biblical times and reasons behind those laments, it will better attune them to examine their own tension-filled realities today. Perhaps it will create "righteous tension" where there is none. Engaging in practices of biblical lament will sharpen the skills of theological reflection in young people so that they will more critically examine our consumeristic culture.

A related concern is the view that youth are merely passive consumers of this culture. As White traces how adolescence has evolved throughout the twentieth century, he contends that pre-Industrialized youth, the time prior to late nineteenth and twentieth centuries, were more involved in the decisions and life of their times. Children passed into adulthood with relative ease since their ability to work determined their status as adults. "The work of pre-industrial young people, while strenuous, was at times fulfilling—connecting them to the earth, their creativity, the care and guidance of adults, and the common good of the community, and affording them a more central social role."[25]

It was not until the Industrial Revolution that child work was considered too harsh, perhaps for very good reasons, and banished from the workplace. However, today's adolescents are delayed entrance into adulthood due to the demands of education, which White argues fits them for the market as producers and consumers. "In contrast with their earlier social roles, youth are now relegated to high schools and to media-driven peer culture that disconnect them from adult care and guidance, the common good, and many of their former contributions and commitments."[26] Even though public tax money could be used for high schools beginning in 1875, it was not until the 1930s that more and more teenagers actually went to high school, thereby delaying a larger

25. White, *Practicing Discernment with Youth*, 15.
26. Ibid., 15.

population's entrance into the adult workforce.[27] Today, one could argue that more and more teenagers are pressured into attending four years of college, and further delaying adulthood.

Preindustrialized youth were anything but passive consumers.[28] Their social roles engaged them in seeking justice and renewal as they engaged in serious work, held significant social roles, and contributed to the social equilibrium. By the mid-twentieth century, however, "good" adolescents were associated with education and "preparation" for adult work and future social significance. White suggests, "While this shift left them without social significance, it provided many with leisure time and discretionary dollars—opening them to exploitation by marketers and their current role as consumers of fashion and entertainment commodities. In one generation that came of age in the 1930s and 1940s, the role of young people shifted from helping to provide for their families to draining their families' income on commodity purchases."[29]

Today, young people are viewed by adults as objects of desire, whether it be the marketing and media giants, or the older adults who want to be young. Adults also view young people with fear. Since the education system has further distanced young people from involvement with adults, many adults may feel that they do not really know those adolescents as real people. This view of youth as objects further instills the relegation of them to be passive because adults do not take their views, beliefs, and opinions seriously. Over time, young people simply learned not to offer their thoughts that may question the status quo, seek justice, or challenge and create new social structures.[30]

Regular engagement with biblical lament will teach young people skills in theological reflection and discernment. It will help them to give voice to possible passivities so that they can begin to take ownership of their life choices, particularly when it affects their "buying power." When practices of lament are done in an

27. Cannister, "Youth Ministry's Historical Context," 82.

28. White, *Practicing Discernment with Youth*, 16.

29. Ibid., 17.

30. Ibid., 18.

intergenerational setting, it will help adults and youth get to know each other as real, authentic people. When people share truthfully from the heart, it seems they are more easily drawn to one another or at least gain a deeper appreciation for the other.

Adolescent Journey

Having overviewed key realities of the cultural landscape, I now turn to specific issues of adolescent faith development. The study of American adolescent development had its start in the late 1800s with noted psychologist G. Stanley Hall. In 1904 he published *Adolescence*[31] in which he pointed out that adolescence was actually a late, prolonged stage of childhood. No longer were they to be thought of as "little adults."[32] He described adolescence as a period of "storm and stress" in which it was a turbulent time charged with conflict and mood swings.[33] Perhaps those thoughts continue to live on today as parents and other adults deal with certain challenges of "teenage rebellion." Overall, we may have the perspective that this is an intensely difficult time of life like no other stage, and so might develop a negative or fearful attitude about these young people.

In the mid-twentieth century Erik Erikson proposed that adolescence was a time in life to determine identity and an ideology. But, a "moratorium" was needed that amounted to a socially approved "time out" so they could complete this quest for an identity and ideology. Erikson developed an eight-stage theory in which humanity matured; the adolescent moratorium was part of stage five and was necessary for overall human development.[34] Today, it seems that as education continues to prepare young people for a future adult life, in which actual "entrance" into adulthood is delayed, "adolescence" is stretched farther into young adulthood. At

---

31. Cannister, "Youth Ministry's Historical Context," 80.
32. Clark, "The Changing Face of Adolescence," 44.
33. Robbins, *This Way to Youth Ministry*, 176.
34. Creasy Dean, *Practicing Passion*, 76.

the same time the average age for onset of puberty dropped from about fifteen years of age a century ago to eleven years of age today. It seems that adolescence is getting both older and younger at the same time.[35]

In time, there would be other "stage theorists" dominating discussions of human development such as Jean Piaget (cognitive development), Lawrence Kohlberg and Carol Gilligan (moral development), and James Fowler (faith development). "Stage theories" became a prominent basis in understanding how people mature. To be sure, these theories of development have been helpful, but they have also been debated and critiqued. Often times these models focus on cognition to the neglect of emotion, on the individual to the neglect of the social, on the stages of development to the neglect of the processes of development, and how a person changes to the neglect of how a person persists.[36] Nevertheless, these views of development greatly influenced the curriculum, activities, and attitudes of twentieth century spiritual caregivers.

In his book, *Sometimes We Wrestle, Sometimes We Dance: Embracing the Spiritual Growth of Adolescents*, Michael Carotta proposes we address spiritual growth in terms of *dimensions* rather than developmental stages.[37] He identifies three dimensions that adult spiritual caregivers can help guide young people: religious faith (vertical), moral living (horizontal), and emotional awareness (internal). Religious faith shapes the way people "see" the God above us, inside others, and within ourselves.[38] It is the way people establish, strengthen, and express their personal relationship with God.[39] Moral living refers to helping young people live a virtuous life of conscience, character, and contribution in both normal and difficult situations.[40] Emotional awareness involves the intrinsic role of emotions in one's behavior, expressions of faith, and moral

35. Clark, "The Changing Face of Adolescence," 45–46.

36. Carotta, *Sometimes We Wrestle, Sometimes We Dance*, 15.

37. Ibid., 15.

38. Ibid., 21.

39. Ibid., 25.

40. Ibid., 27.

interactions. There is a relationship between one's ability to manage emotions and one's ability to demonstrate responsible behavior.[41]

As adult spiritual caregivers walk with and guide youth in these three dimensions of spiritual growth, Carotta suggests five characteristics of adolescent spirituality: friendship, prayer, mystery, doubt, and gratitude. He states, " . . . the adolescent challenge to make sense of things and to find meaning in the ironies of life results in a strong and natural desire for a spirituality that touches almost all the aspects of an adolescent's life. Adolescents possess a spirituality that touches the athletic field, preparation for exams, the grieving over a tragic death, the stress of problem-solving, the fear of rejection, the pain of failure, and the joy of dreams fulfilled."[42]

Biblical lament is a form of prayer that welcomes mystery and doubt, and usually leads to praise and gratitude. It fosters friendship between God and themselves in ways that are open, authentic, and transparent. If done appropriately within the safe context of a group guided by adult spiritual caregivers, it nurtures trust among the group and with the adult role model. Lament shapes the way young people see God and ultimately the type of religious faith that Carotta suggests. Engaging in lament helps young people become emotionally aware as they identify their internal feelings that will impact their moral living and how they live out their faith.

Three Adolescent Longings

Kenda Creasy Dean, professor of youth, church, and culture, suggests three basic longings of adolescents—fidelity, transcendence, communion—in her book *Practicing Passion: Youth and the Quest for a Passionate Church*. She asserts that youth are full of passion and looking for something to die for, thus making it worth living for.[43] The current church in the United States, particularly in her

41. Ibid., 25.
42. Ibid., 19.
43. Creasy Dean, *Practicing Passion*, 2.

United Methodist tradition, has become passionless.[44] Passionate youth will not be attracted to a passionless church. The church needs to awaken itself to its passions, yet not just to any passion but the identified Passion of Christ and God's passion. In that passion the church will better be able to understand its true identity.

Adolescents live out and explore many different passions; some are harmful. They too need to understand and experience the Passion of Christ as they mature in their identity. But again, she suggests the Mainline church has not aided the youth in this manner, and argues that "theology" is the weak link.[45] For far too long the Protestant Church has depended upon social science to understand and interpret "adolescence" in order to help them. Erikson's stage theory emphasized a "moratorium" for adolescents to understand who they are and what they will become.[46] However, Creasy Dean suggests that the landscape has changed from when Erikson formulated his theories in the mid-twentieth century. Today, adults desire to be youth and external forces on youth do not allow for a moratorium. This "moratorium" has all but vanished[47] given that young people are no longer in the same contact with adults as had once been, which was critical for adolescents to complete their identity according to Erikson.[48] Ultimately, she contends that high school aged adolescents are generally not ready to be faithful to a lifelong ideology.[49]

Maturity is no longer a result of a "grown up adolescent." Rather, self-fulfillment is the cultural emphasis. Creasy Dean turns to theology to help the church understand its true role. She suggests that in ministering to young people in their search to attach to something to die for, this will enable the church to better serve and minister to all people. Ministry is ministry, regardless of the

44. Ibid., 15.
45. Ibid., 9 and 83.
46. Ibid., 12–14.
47. Ibid., 81.
48. Ibid., 78.
49. Ibid., 76.

age, and therefore can be both formative and informative to all parts of the church.

The passion found among adolescents shows itself by three overarching longings, that of fidelity, transcendence, and communion. Passion seeks fidelity and the ability to be faithful. They want to know, "Will you be there for me?" "Before adolescents can take seriously the gospel's claim that Jesus will 'be there' always, a community of affirming others must 'be there' for them, demonstrating steadfast love on their behalf." [50] However, this should not be perceived that adult spiritual caregivers need to make themselves available to young people every waking hour of every week; this is a real danger in adolescent ministry. "Being there" includes them learning of the fidelity of God and the entire faith community, not just with certain individuals.[51]

As we engage in the practice of biblical lament with young people, they will grow in their understanding of God's fidelity and Christ's passion for them, and deepen their own fidelity to God and Christ. Afterall, the foundation of biblical lament is that God is there for God's people, ever-listening and ever-accompanying humanity in life. The honest and transparent conversation of lament enables young people to know that nothing can be said that will tarnish God's fidelity to them, thereby increasing their fidelity to God. As Old Testament scholar Kathleen O'Conner writes, "Although laments appear disruptive of God's world, they are acts of fidelity. In vulnerability and honesty, they cling to God and demand for God to see, hear, and act . . . in the process of harsh complaint and resistance, they also express faith in God in the midst of chaos, doubt, and confusion."[52]

The second longing experience of young people is that for transcendence. They yearn for ecstasy, an emotional or physical "high." The question among adolescents is, "Did it move me?" and "[as] a result, adolescents tend to consider *any* moving personal experience, from roller coasters to orgasms, potentially 'spiritual.'

50. Ibid., 77.

51. Ibid., 90.

52. O'Conner, *Lamentations and the Tears of the World*, 9.

Indeed, in both primitive time and in ours, people have often viewed moving experience to be what religion is *for*."[53] As a theological response to this longing, Creasy Dean acknowledges that the mystery of God may address the adolescent's "need to be moved ecstatically beyond borders of self to a posture of awe."[54] Young people today do not view mystery as a problem to be solved as much as a truth to be revealed in the course of human experience.

This point of a demand for experience connects with Carol Lytch's study in *Choosing Church: What Makes a Difference for Teens*. It was mentioned earlier that Lytch found teens were attracted to churches who offered them a sense of belonging, a sense of meaning, and opportunities to develop competence. But Lytch also discovered that in order to foster a longer-lasting, durable sense that they would continue in the church after they left home involved two movements, that of religious socialization and religious experience. Both *religious socialization* and *religious experience* are needed for teens to develop a mature faith. She defines "socialization" as the larger process that builds the knowledge of the symbols, rituals, narratives, texts, and habits, and "experience" as those times when teens reported an encounter with God.[55] Lytch writes:

> The connection between having a religious experience and developing religious loyalty is seen best when it is juxtaposed with my findings on consistent religious socialization. The unshakable loyalists, those with the highest degree of loyalty to the religious tradition, had both religious experience and consistent socialization . . . socialization conditions persons to have religious experiences by providing them with the symbols, stories, and practices to use for 'sifting' their experiences and interpreting them as religious . . . socialization and religious experience work together in a circular fashion."[56]

---

53. Creasy Dean, *Practicing Passion*, 99.

54. Ibid., 103.

55. Lytch, *Choosing Church*, 58–59.

56. Ibid., 61–62.

Religious experiences, those powerful encounters with God, often happen to young people when they go on retreats or service projects, or when they are away from their everyday environment. They can occur at conventions, camps, or charged up concerts, where the pulsating music of the band and large crowds help move them. It can also happen when the words of a dynamic speaker connect with them in a unique way, or in the quiet moments by the still lake waters of a moonlit evening at camp. Religious socialization, on the other hand, refers to the mundane and ritualistic aspect of religious life, like going to church every Sunday, regular devotions, habitual prayers before meals, annual winter youth retreats, and monthly service projects. It can also refer to the intentional efforts and structured practices by a group to pass on their beliefs and faith traditions to others through such attempts as catechism, Sunday school material, and weekly activities.

Biblical lament welcomes the mysterious aspects of faith. It is important for us to recall that in many lament Psalms there was a sudden and unexplained turn in the flow. After naming the ills of life or the mistreatment of God or the injustices that abounded, the psalmist offered praise to God. There is no explanation for how or why the "vow of praise" happens. As Walter Brueggemann points out, "We cannot ever know whether it is changed circumstance, or changed attitude, or something of both. But the speaker now speaks differently. Now the sense of urgency and desperation is replaced with joy, gratitude, and well-being."[57] This is indeed a mysterious reality of biblical lament. Perhaps the authors had some sort of religious experience or encounter with God that moved them in ways that eventually led to praise.

The third longing of passionate youth is communion, a yearning for the union with the source of their delight.[58] This expression of intimacy is about attachment. It is closely related to the longings of fidelity and transcendence. The desire for intimacy is rooted in the strong bond between an infant and the mother. "Securely attached children are more sociable, self-reliant, curious,

57. Brueggemann, *The Message of the Psalm*, 56.
58. Creasy Dean, *Practicing Passion*, 117.

and involved than their peers; having experienced empathy themselves, they have a greater capacity to display it to others."[59] Intimacy carries with it the gift of "being known" by another and
thereby developing trust. "If transcendence draws young people
beyond the confines of self, communion invites them to live
radically *within* the boundaries of being human, starting with
their own bodies."[60]

Practices of biblical lament call us to bear our true selves to
God and opening us up to God's true self as well. It is within la-
ment where our utter naked pain, suffering, and shame is revealed.
We are invited by God to loosen the boundaries and walls of
separation, even in the most intimate details of our life and grief.
Pastoral theologian Robert Dykstra argues that the rending of the
Jewish Temple curtain immediately after Jesus' death on the cross
(Mark 15:38; Matthew 27:51) signifies the unveiling of God. "The
One who was hidden, the unknown and unknowable God, is sud-
denly now revealed."[61] This act of divine self-exposure is linked
with divine lament and stands in striking contrast to the strong
prohibitions against seeing God's body throughout the Hebrew
scriptures.[62] In response to Jesus' death and out of the unbearable
grief, shame, and rage experienced by God, God's lament drives
God to expose Godself to humanity in ways not previously done.
This vulnerable act of naked aggression tears the old division between the sacred and profane.[63]

So far this chapter has been about "adolescence" in general,
broad considerations. However, it is important to remember that
each young person is unique and develops differently from others,
even if there are some overarching similarities and longings. It is
vital that we not overgeneralize and treat young people as "statistics" or "developmental categories." Nevertheless, we as adult spiritual caregivers can gain much insight by learning of these various

59. Ibid., 118.

60. Ibid., 120.

61. Dykstra, "Rending the Curtain," 59.

62. Ibid., 60.

63. Ibid., 62.

adolescent developmental considerations. Since adolescence in the United States seems to be "getting younger" and "growing older" at the same time, I will now examine more specifically some of the characteristics and considerations among early (ages 10-14), middle (ages 13-19), and late adolescents (ages 18-25+). The ages listed are solely meant for descriptive purposes, since there is obviously some overlap among what ages fall within which category. However, it is also important to keep in mind that the life situation of a young person may better explain why they may be demonstrating certain behaviors or characteristics not in their particular sub-stage of adolescence. In other words, it is very possible for some twenty year olds to demonstrate characteristics of early adolescence and some thirteen year olds to seemingly function like late adolescents.

Early Adolescence

For early adolescents, the impact of the onset of puberty cannot be overstated. They are being transformed, not simply transitioned from childhood to adulthood.[64] Becoming more self-conscious, they vie for peer friendships in ways that did not matter to them in pre-adolescence.[65] These young people are just beginning to explore the issue of identity, even though theirs is still firmly fixed within the context of the family system.[66] Adult spiritual caregivers can nurture these junior highers by helping them build supportive peer friendships, by facilitating learning activities that emphasize "doing faith" in response to God's love, by offering them meaningful relationships with adults, by creating opportunities for them to make contributions that highlight their individual value to others, and by communicating clear moral boundaries and behavioral expectations.[67]

---

64. Dunn, 171.

65. Ibid., 173–174.

66. Clark, "The Changing Face of Adolescence," 56.

67. Dunn, 176–179.

Biblical lament may be a bit stretching for some early adolescents, particularly in regards to "getting angry" with God. Depending on what they were taught growing up, anger towards God may violate a moral value. Therefore, other aspects of biblical lament may need to be emphasized to make it "age appropriate." They could be encouraged to simply name their anger, regardless of the source, as the first step in lament. Nevertheless, engaging biblical lament with a group of junior highers can help facilitate supportive, caring peer friendships, particularly if they share their anger, frustrations, confusions, and questions with each other. Then they will know that they are not alone in this beginning, transformative phase of the adolescent journey. Writing their own laments is a practical, tangible learning activity that ultimately lets them know of their value in the sight of God and caring adult spiritual leaders. Even though practicing biblical lament with this age group may be challenging for some, if done well, it can create a foundation of communicating with God and other people that will serve them well as they grow older.

Middle Adolescence

Issues involving peer groups and friendships will probably dominate the lives of middle adolescents.[68] It may be that even though family support is still present for these young people, it will seldom be claimed by them. They may not express a desire to spend time with their parents, but there is a desire for them to know that their parents are available when they want them.[69] Middle adolescents are exploring more of who they are becoming and it is often through other people they consider who they themselves are as they pay close attention to what others say about them. They possess a deep felt need for affirmation and acceptance.[70] Adult spiritual caregivers can mentor senior highers toward authenticity and depth in their

---

68. Ibid., 188.

69. Clark, "The Changing Face of Adolescence," 56.

70. Dunn, *Shaping the Spiritual Life of Students*, 192.

close relationships, assist them in learning to own and appropriately express their emotions, model maturity in moral skills and reasoning, and provide direct feedback, support, and challenge as they further establish their identities as children of God.[71]

Engaging in biblical lament with this age group can help them navigate their emotional ups and downs related to ever-evolving friendships, identity struggles, and parental challenges. Biblical lament can help them identify their internal emotions and assist them in appropriately dealing with them, thereby leading toward a deeper and more authentic relationship not only with God but also with people around them. Lament will shape their view of God as one who cares and will be faithful to them, even if there is intense anger and frustration within their lives. Middle adolescents may be able to handle certain "paradoxical tensions" of getting angry with God and then praising God than would early adolescents, but they will still need much adult mentoring to express themselves in such ways. Adults who model biblical lament will help give these young people permission to do so themselves.

Late Adolescence

Of all the three sub-stages of adolescence addressed in this chapter, late adolescence is perhaps the most complex and diverse. Upon graduation or dropping out of high school, life can go a variety of directions for them. Some get jobs or get married, while others go on to college or graduate school and do not engage in certain traditional markers of adulthood until later in life. Even if emerging adults get married or have children or purchase a home, it is no guarantee that they are adequately prepared for the accompanying responsibilities. Unlike early and middle adolescents, who for the most part are either in junior or senior high, late adolescents who do not go further in their formal education may no longer have a structure of adult spiritual caregivers walking with them. This contributes to the ambiguity and uncertainty of when a young adult

71. Ibid., 194–198.

actually reaches "adulthood" and not be considered an adolescent by society any more.

Nevertheless, no matter which journey late adolescents take after high school, many will grapple with issues related to intimate companionship, a compelling life vision, a coherent worldview, and a composition of commitments.[72] "Older adolescents stand on the threshold of making their mark on society and community but are often held back by systemic and environmental factors—parents who empower sloth and financial dependency, an educational system that treats the undergraduate curriculum as barely adequate preparation for graduate school, and media and advertising industries that make a far larger profit by appealing to the young to stay young (and the old to fight aging), to name a few."[73]

Perhaps the most influential gift that an adult spiritual caregiver can offer these young people is that of mentoring and simply being there for them as their identity struggles evolve. The power of a mentoring relationship is that they can help anchor the vision of the late adolescent by offering emotional support, insight, and challenge. "In a healthy mentoring relationship, the emerging adult neither worships the mentor as a hero nor needs to push off counterdependently. Rather, he or she is appropriately dependent upon a chosen (self-selected) 'Authority out there' to beckon and confirm the integrity emerging from within."[74] The mentor confers recognition in powerful and practical terms,[75] and can extend the hospitality to ask big enough questions that will lead to a worthy faith, bearing the test of a lived experience in a real world.[76]

Again, as young adults try on certain adult roles for the first time in their lives and experience even more new-found freedoms, they will continue the ups and downs of these lived out changes. Engaging in biblical lament can help name and identify their confusions, doubts, and frustrations as they struggle with intimacy,

72. Ibid., 209.

73. Clark, "The Changing Face of Adolescence," 57.

74. Daloz Parks, *Big Questions, Worthy Dreams*, 106.

75. Ibid., 167.

76. Ibid., 33.

identity, and vocational issues. Perhaps some of the authors of biblical or personal laments may serve as literary mentors to them. But as important as modeling the engagement of biblical lament by adult spiritual caregivers is for early and middle adolescents, for late adolescents this demonstration will take on greater significance because it helps them know more of the caregiver's personal story of faith and life. These emerging adults may now be grappling with similar life issues and will need assurance from others who have already traversed this journey.

Conclusion

Discernment

As noted in the introduction of this chapter, David White suggests that the future of youth ministry must include efforts that equip young people and their congregations with skills for bringing the gospel into creative tension with questions and circumstances for our lives. He contends that practicing discernment needs to be an inclusive rhythm of life.[77] Discernment is a language of the heart, mind, soul, and body. White offers a four-step method to reclaim the Christian practice of discernment. The first step makes our heart sensitive to the Spirit by focusing on affect and intuition. The second step recognizes that God speaks to us through our mind; we must engage in intellectual analysis. The third step privileges contemplation and biblical/theological imagination through remembering and dreaming. The fourth step challenges us to put the previous efforts into action.

By engaging these practices youth will internalize ideas, sensibilities, and commitments that will direct their future choices and help them learn wisdom from these practical movements. Rather than simply pass on information and knowledge to young people, this method creates a conversation between adults, Christian traditions, and youth. While exploring truth about ourselves, our world, and God, we will become aware of the potential

77. White, *Practicing Discernment with Youth*, xii.

distortions of other life practices. White says, "The practice of discernment assumes that God seeks to lead people to greater fullness and faithfulness."[78]

The first step of discernment is listening to our hearts. It is a means of resisting forces that distract us from desires appropriate to our humanity from love of God and neighbor.[79] Our society is full of "hard-hearted" people. The first step of reclaiming a "hard heart" is to grieve.[80] Only then will we be able to more adequately cultivate feelings that are appropriate to our situation. As we discern where God is working we will also experience internal healing. I believe this sharpens the skills of empathy and self-awareness while we get a realistic view of life.

Lament is one obvious prayer resource that will help adolescents grieve and soften their hard hearts. Practicing lament will help them become more self-aware and empower their empathetic skills. In addition, Michael Jinkins points out that performing practices of lament offers people a language that recognizes God as Sovereign. Inhabiting this language sensitizes them to such a theocentric worldview[81] and foster a God-honoring heart. Habitual practice of lament will shape their character and heart in ways that discern the sacred quality of life, both in themselves and of other people.

The second step is to seek understanding by using our minds and intellect. White contends that our current educational efforts drain youth and averts them from wanting to learn.[82] It is no wonder that Sunday school or any type of Bible study that employs use of the intellect is not readily accepted by most youth because they are tired of learning. Theologically, White draws upon biblical wisdom spirituality that focuses on the discovery of the world, as a means of discernment and learning.[83] This exploration of the

---

78. Ibid., 65.

79. Ibid., 91.

80. Ibid., 96.

81. Jinkins, *In the House of the Lord*, 3.

82. White, *Practicing Discernment with Youth*, 115.

83. Ibid., 118.

world and the practices that we do in life fosters discernment in ways that the disclosure stories of the Torah and disruption antics of the Prophets do not generate.

Biblical lament is dialogical and embodies conversation between God and humanity. This dialogue possesses no answers that need to be learned, but demonstrates a way of communicating with God. Even though lament sharpens our ability to engage our emotions, it also calls us to use our minds to articulate ourselves and God's possible response. Furthermore, since biblical laments function as acts of persuasion exhorting God to act on behalf of the innocent, the victim, and the suffering, it requires our minds to speak to God in passionate ways that seek to move God to action.[84] Encouraging youth to personalize their own biblical laments will instill in them a learning style that is interactive, dynamic, and dialogical rather than solely mastering information presented to them in a unidirectional manner.

The third step involves loving God with our soul by remembering and dreaming. One of White's critiques is that our culture fosters both fragmentation and alienation of our youth.[85] And so by remembering the "God story" youth can see their part in it, but then by dreaming, they can further discover their role in the active participation of it. Young people, suggests White, have a prophetic vocation primarily due to the developmental nature of their age and their drive towards coherence of life.[86] Youth are always striving to make sense of their reality. The Torah stories can help them engage in the contradictions of the world. Grounded in the biblical story, it can help youth to dream about an alternative perspective for how life ought to be. Remembering and dreaming gives us a sense of Christian identity and brings about healing when we connect our lives to the life of God. In this way, commercial culture is devoid of a sense of history, which fosters loneliness and isolation for youth.

---

84. Brown and Miller, "Introduction," xv.

85. White, *Practicing Discernment with Youth*, 141.

86. Ibid., 148.

Located within the structure of the lament itself is the expectation for young people to remember those times of God's faithfulness. After naming the painful reality and recalling of God's salvific ways, youth are led to eventually offer authentic praise. Recalling previous ways that God delivered them will provoke their imagination to consider God's creative means of future grace and countless possibilities of its expression. The first and second chapters of Lamentations reveal an objective narrator turned compassionate advocate. Practices of lament will sensitize adolescents for similar advocacy and intercessory work on behalf of others who find themselves helpless and suffering.

The fourth step involves loving God with our strength and body by living out our beliefs and theological reflections. White suggests that the need is not for youth to take on more activity in life since they already engage in many activities, but notes there is a lack of meaningful activity due to entertainment models that lull youth into passive consumption.[87] By participating in non-reflective activities, White suggests that we are then supporting the status quo that prefers that young people "sleep." God's reign, however, calls us to action.

Lament demands theological reflection and critical engagement with the realities of this world. It refuses denial and decries concealment of stories of suffering, but rather puts forth an expression of faithfulness that gives voice to suffering, empowers one to persuade God to act in just and righteous ways, and challenges us to a life of compassionate advocacy and intercession on behalf of the weak and oppressed. Lament fosters and demands a faith that is dynamic and active, not static and stagnant. Nevertheless, practicing biblical lament will require our youth to slow down and not allow the high speed pace of our American culture to dominate their lives. Inhabiting lament in our daily lives will sharpen our skills of discernment and reflection. Lament will shape identity and meaning as they journey the path of adolescence from junior high through young adulthood.

---

87. Ibid., 176.

6

Other Ways to Engage Biblical Lament

Why so much stress, O Lord?

*So many decisions hang over my head, and I can't
find relief until they're gone and over.*

*Trying to find time to relax has been way
too difficult, leaving me exhausted.*

*There has always been things for me to stress about, whether
it was friends, relationships, work, school and much more,
but yet you have always brought me through.*

*Thank you so much Lord that even in the midst of all
the busyness of my days and stress that I encounter,
you still pull me through.*

*Everything will pass, and that gives me hope to face
the next issue.*

— EMERGING ADULT

OBVIOUSLY THERE ARE MORE ways to engage biblical lament
with young people than the three-step, six-minute, timed-writing
prayer exercise detailed in chapter 3. Though it has its limitations,

a strength of it is that it can be a helpful introduction to the genre of biblical lament. In this chapter, I offer additional ideas in how to engage biblical lament with young people in both variations of this specific prayer exercise and how other important faith practices can incorporate lament.

Variations of the Prayer Exercise

At its basic level, the practice in chapter 3 involves a young person spending six minutes writing out their prayer of lament in three two-minute steps. This can be done alone or in a setting where other people are writing their own prayers.

One simple variation is to use this prayer exercise as a form of intercessory prayer. Rather than writing about their own grief and anger, a person can pray on behalf of a friend or other group of people. When I have introduced this prayer exercise to people and before we actually began, someone inevitably said that they were not in a particularly "lamentful mood" or were not sure what to personally be angry about. In those situations I invited them to write on someone else's behalf. Perhaps they had a friend or family member who was going through a tough time. Maybe they were aware of a group of people suffering from some injustice. In those moments, they were invited to be "compassionate advocates" like the person in Lamentations chapters 1 and 2.

In the same vein, you could have youth write about a common topic or theme suggested by you. Perhaps you led a Bible study or faith discussion on a particular place in the world or issue. Then, you could follow-up by having youth focus their lament around that particular location or reality. This also serves as an expression of intercessory prayer, but what is different than the previous paragraph is that everyone's prayerful attention is focused on the same general thought rather than on their own personal pain or anger. Or similarly, have them write a communal lament on behalf of one of the communities to which they belong, such as their church, youth group, family, school, etc. This imitates the few corporate laments found in the Psalms.

Another variation is to adjust the amount of time. In my project, some younger adults expressed they would have appreciated more time reflecting than the allotted six minutes. Rather than two minutes per step, make it three or four minutes or however long seems appropriate. Or, if you are leading a longer weekend or day long retreat on loss or grief, have each person spend one hour or two hours per step either in one sitting or spread out over the retreat's duration.

Rather than writing individually, have two people work together on a joint prayer of lament. This fosters conversation between them as they agree together in what to write down. They could write of a shared experience or from the perspective of their faith or school communities. Time will need to be lengthened for each step. And, you could tell them in advance that these joint prayers will all be read to the rest of the group. Again, this becomes more of a corporate prayer experience than a solitary one. It can be quite powerful to hear the words of prayers written by others.

Instead of writing, have them draw their prayer by either portraying three distinct images or developing the same picture as they are guided through each of the three steps. They could also mold clay or playdough or utilize some other artful medium that engages the right brain. In my project, there were a few people who had some learning disabilities. For them writing was a hindrance to expressing their lament. If this is done in a group setting and if they are comfortable doing so, youth could be invited to share about their drawing, painting, or sculpture with others. This too turns a private prayer into a communal experience.

Youth could be encouraged to practice lament outside of the youth group or church setting. For example, they could write lyrics to a song, a poem, a short story or create a video based on the framework of biblical lament and present their pieces to the rest of the youth group at some common time. Similarly, they could be given a "homework assignment" that includes identifying some other author's song, poem, short story, or video that captures well the sentiment of their own feelings of lament. Later, they could bring these back to the group explaining how their artifact connects well to either their own personal lament or the lament of their peers or some other group of people.

Young people could be inspired to engage lament as part of their own private devotional time. They could keep these in a personal prayer journal. Or perhaps during Lent or other times of the year, youth could be challenged to write a lament daily or weekly over a set time period. This may seem overwhelming at first, but journaling in this focused way may prove helpful, particularly if this is a shared, group experience.

Conduct an entire worship service using the basic three-step structure of biblical lament. This gets beyond people writing out their prayers, but guides them through each phase. I once led a "Service of Hymns and Scripture" chapel at our college. The opening call to worship introduced biblical lament to the gathered body, followed by three sections of crying out to God, remembering God's goodness, and praising God. Each segment included scripture passages and songs specific to each step.

Similarly, if one uses lament as a theme for a weekend or day-long retreat, you could spend longer blocks of time having them reflect, journal, or participate in some other corporate worship activity for each act. I have led several weekend retreats with junior and senior high youth where I engaged biblical lament with them. For one retreat I employed the theme "Jesus, Prayer, and You." Though not all four of the teaching and worship sessions engaged lament, I did focus the third session on it. I shared how Jesus' own Jewish spirituality practiced lament and that he quoted Psalm 22 as he hung on the cross in his hour of need. Then, I led them in the six-minute, timed-writing prayer exercise. It was an opportunity to once again demonstrate to young people that God truly wants to hear honestly from us. At a different retreat, I focused on the spirituality of the Psalms for the four worship times. The first session overviewed the book, and the next three sessions engaged the psalms of well-being, disorientation, and new orientation as described by Walter Brueggemann in *Spirituality of the Psalms* (Minneapolis: Fortress Press, 2002). In such retreat settings, I like to introduce and practice lament alongside other types of prayer so that the whole weekend is not solely focused on lament when other fun games and activities are also happening. In this way, there is not as much of a disconnect between the worship sessions and the rest of the retreat happenings.

The next two ideas, Bible study and preaching, could be reserved for the next section since they are forms of "faith practices," but I wish to highlight them here. As a youth group, you could study biblical characters of lament. Not only does this model to young people about others who lamented, but we learn more about the narrative and why God received those prayers. This reinforces the biblical perspective of lament. Another way to engage lament with the faith community is to preach about lament from the pulpit. Not only will youth hear this message, but so will the entire congregation. This too will educate a faith community about the important role and function of biblical lament as necessary for a holistic individual and corporate relationship with God.

Faith Practices Engaging Lament

After offering some variations of the three-step, timed-writing prayer exercise, I will now suggest why it is important for some other faith practices to somehow incorporate lament. First, let me explain by what I mean by "practices." Christian practices are "things Christian people do together over time to address fundamental human needs in response to and in the light of God's active presence for the life of the world."[1] Such practices combine both thought and action, and cannot be separated from one another as they work to usher in the values of God's reign. They stem from fundamental human needs and conditions, but are also social, historical activities that people engage in over time. Christian practices share in the mysterious dynamic of fall and grace, of sin and redemption, and may issue a profound awareness and deep knowing of the knowledge of God and creation.[2] Ultimately, such

1. Dykstra and Bass, "A Theological Understanding of Christian Practices," 18.

2. Ibid., 22–27.

practices assist us with theological reflection in the midst of our daily lives. The practices I will now focus on include rituals, rites of passage, turning points, story-telling, and story-making.

Rituals

"Rituals can be generally described as patterned activities that create and express meaning through the use of symbols and gestures . . . [they] make statements about what we believe about life and ourselves, even when we are not fully conscious that they are doing so."[3] They can range from the more elaborate activities that we do in church (i.e. communion, weddings, baptisms) to the more mundane, everyday activities (i.e. praying while enjoying a morning cup of coffee, a simple family prayer before meals). Rituals lift up an event, heighten its expectancy, make it special, and can assist us in moving through life's painful losses, or deepen our joyful experiences.[4] Activities that we give intentional, deliberate thought to, as well as those that stem from the unconscious or habitual routines are rituals. Done in both individual and communal settings, they bring familiarity, comfort, security, and organized routine.

Why should we do rituals with our youth? In a church setting, one purpose is to help bring about spiritual transformation and spiritual growth as individuals seek to be disciples of Jesus Christ. They help our youth develop identity, purpose, and meaning, and build community while connecting our personal narratives with those of our family, school, church, and culture. Rituals create memories and stories, and can help adolescents make wise choices. Ritualizing our stories fosters group identity and provides the foundation for being an individual (meaning-making). Stories possess the power to construct meaning and communicate ourselves to others.[5] Communicating ourselves to others requires articulation, and when it comes to articulating our faith,

---

3. Oswald, *Transforming Rituals*, 11.

4. Hogue, *Remembering the Future, Imagining the Past*, 122.

5. Anderson and Foley, *Mighty Stories, Dangerous Rituals*, 4.

the National Study of Youth and Religion contends that American teenagers (and adults!) struggle with this.

Utilizing rituals that involve biblical lament in the context of group worship can further help young people come in contact with the transformative power of God as their own bodies and minds are changing during adolescence. Biblical lament connects young people with the ongoing God-story and Christian faith tradition, while also providing an avenue to make meaning of this story within the context of their own life, struggles, and joys. Group rituals involving lament help to form a faith community together that is built on openness with each other while serving as a safe place to share the ups and downs of life. Furthermore, such rituals will heighten, bless, and authenticate the very real experience of adolescents as they struggle with issues of faith, doubt, and uncertainties.

Malidoma Somé is a West African native of the Dagara culture. He has been called by his village elders to devote himself to speak about and conduct workshops on ritual. His job is to help interpret and explain to the modern culture his tribal world, and vice versa. Somé's book, *Ritual: Power, Healing, and Community*, describes the role and purpose of ritual in the Dagara culture, particularly those focusing on death and grief. For the Dagara, ritual is the yardstick by which people measure their state of connection with the hidden ancestral realm. Abandonment of ritual can be devastating.[6]

There are various dimensions of ritual, including communal, familial, and individual, which are interdependent of one another. To remember how to perform ritualistic activities we must slow down. One of Somé's major critiques of the West and industrial world is its dependence on speed. Ritual, he contends, is not compatible with such a rapid rhythm of life.[7] "The West is a 'showoff' culture that intimidates,"[8] declares Somé, "and the Machine

---

6. Somé, *Ritual*, 12.

7. Ibid., 15–17.

8. Ibid., 39–40.

culture is a violent break away from the realm of the spirit."[9] If rituals are done for "show" purposes, they will lose their power and effectiveness. Whatever happens in a ritual space, some kind of power is released if given freedom in which to live. He suggests that each time we enter ritual space it is because something in the physical world has warned us of possible deterioration at hand.[10] Therefore, we enter ritual in order to respond to the call of the soul. The success of a ritual depends on the purpose of the individuals involved in it.[11] Since ritual is a collaborative effort between humans and the spirit world, our role in ritual is to be human.[12]

Keeping Somé's perspectives in mind, rituals involving biblical lament can empower young people to slow down for reflection of life's happenings in the midst of their busyness. This may be a particular challenge for adolescents since times for silence are sparse. Nevertheless, this is an important requirement of developing a mature faith that critically and theologically engages this world.

As we live into the future where the rate of change continues to speed up, this acceleration forces us to make social readjustments. Young people today may have trouble coping with all the cumulative effects of this change. Roy Oswald says that as we go through these transitions and changes, we need to come to terms with these new situations.[13] Transitions begin with an ending, and then move into a neutral zone where there is a time of confusion, fear, doubt, struggle, and waiting, until it finally concludes with a new beginning. Oswald contends that rituals can aid this three-phase process of transition. When done well, rituals can foster a deeper surrendered life in God through spiritual growth and spiritual transformation.[14] The congregation's role in developing a ritualized life is to help individuals and families, congregations, and the wider community engage in activities that lead to a

9. Ibid., 45.

10. Ibid., 25.

11. Ibid., 27.

12. Ibid., 32.

13. Oswald, *Transforming Rituals*, 4.

14. Ibid., 6.

further surrendering to God. In ministering through rituals, the faith community and the adult spiritual caregiver's roles among adolescents is to teach and coach, encourage and support, model, advocate, and evaluate.[15]

For healing to occur, professor of pastoral theology and counseling David Hogue argues "that rituals are critical to healing and transformation."[16] He asserts that historically people often listened to the stories of other people, but paid little attention to the rituals of their lives. Rituals are perhaps most often thought of as occurring in worship, but they also occur in our families, schools, sports teams, or other private settings that structure our day and life. "Most rituals have been developed over time as safe havens from the stress of life or ways to deal with life changes."[17] Hogue indicates that "rituals assist us in *moving* through life's painful losses as well as *deepening* our experience of our joys . . . They can help us overcome the 'stuckness' of experiences, attitudes, or circumstances that seem to hold onto us and keep us from moving ahead."[18]

Rituals that celebrate joyous occasions such as weddings, high school graduations, and believer's baptisms or confirmations can be containers for mixed feelings. In spite of the movement toward something good, there is still loss in the transition. Youth will say good-bye to high school friends and their parents as they go to college or voluntary service. Junior high students who go onto a bigger high school setting may feel lost in the crowd and yearn for the smaller setting of junior high. Those who get married will soon realize that their previous lifestyles and patterns will change to accommodate this new and wonderful relationship. At its best, the ritual space will provide a safe setting for the conflicting feelings of joy and sorrow. Biblical lament can help people name their fears, struggles, and losses along with their excitements, blessings, and gains during significant ritualistic events in their lives.

---

15. Ibid., 8–9.

16. Hogue, *Remembering the Future, Imagining the Past*, 120.

17. Ibid., 121.

18. Ibid., 122.

Rites of passage

"Rites of passages are valuable but imperfect ways of enacting meaning,"[19] writes Ronald Grimes, author of *Deeply Into the Bone: Re-Inventing Rites of Passage*. They are "stylized and condensed actions intended to acknowledge or effect a transformation. A transformation is not just any sort of change but a momentous metamorphosis, a moment after which one is never again the same."[20] Grimes contends there is a global problem today with an absence of coming of age initiation rites.[21] The lack of these leads to a breakdown in the maturation process. He also admits that the problem is not simply the lack of compelling initiations but that the existing ones are dysfunctional. As initiation rites are reinvented, they will provide for opportunities of maturation. These events must ensure that we attend fully to the spiritual, psychological, and social aspects of our human selves, or else they risk becoming a yawning abyss that drains energy and creates social confusion.[22]

Traditionally, rites of passages in other cultures have included a three-stage structure: a preliminal (separation) phase, a marginal or liminal phase, and a postliminal (reincorporation phase).[23] During the separation phase, young people are physically removed from the communities in which they live as children. This disrupts them from all the routines and structures that support their identity as children. The second step, the liminal phase, encourages children to step across the threshold from childhood to adulthood. These former-children-not-yet-adults are often immersed in an unfamiliar and frightening period that may last for days or weeks. "To make the critical transition from one life stage to another, one must dramatically, forcefully, and sometimes painfully leave behind former ways of being, earlier ways of experiencing

19. Grimes, *Deeply Into the Bone*, 336.

20. Ibid., 6.

21. Ibid., 91.

22. Ibid., 5.

23. Hogue, *Remembering the Future, Imagining the Past*, 127; Grimes, *Deeply Into the Bone*, 6.

oneself. To be transformed, one must live with an extended period of deep uncertainty."[24] The final step involves the reincorporation stage, where the former children are now returned to their communities as adults. "They enter a new stage of learning and formation in which they live into the new roles for which they have been preparing."[25]

There are few rites in the American church that recognize a "coming of age," particularly to the degree described in the previous paragraph. However, if churches neglect such rites of passage, Grimes contends that young people will engage in ritualizing practices or activities that impact their maturation in unhealthy manners. In other words, in a young person's search for meaning, they will explore areas reserved for adulthood whether the church is proactively helping them or not; some of these activities may be destructive or harmful, such as drug or alcohol abuse.[26] As churches employ the use of rites of passage in the adolescent journey, the role of lament can help them process and bring to God their fears, questions, and doubts along with their joys and excitements. The structure of biblical lament has a flow to it that may mimic the movement of a rite of passage. Since lament psalms are categorized as those of disorientation, [27] these may resonate with youth who are in the throes of a liminal reality.

Turning Points

Turning points are times in a person's life when decisive change takes place.[28] Adolescence is comprised of numerous turning points or transitions that youth experience. This time of life is ripe for them to recognize the many ways God is present. Marcey Balcomb and Kevin Witt suggest that "[a] twist of *fate* can be

24. Hogue, *Remembering the Future, Imagining the Past*, 128.

25. Ibid., 128.

26. Grimes, *Deeply Into the Bone*, 94.

27. Brueggemann, *Spirituality of the Psalms*, 25.

28. Balcomb and Witt, *Twists of Faith*, 9.

transformed into a twist of *faith*."[29] Youth tend to know God is with them through their experiences of life and will recall memories more readily when they are tied to strong emotions; times of transition may insight such memories. Therefore, it is crucial that adults help young people reflect and unpack their various experiences in order to better see the hand of God. What is needed are adults who are spiritually mature in their own faith; not simply activity directors. Mature spiritual mentors are able to work in the transition zones of young people and aid them in their own journey of faith development.[30]

This concept of "turning points" is similar to that of rites of passage, yet deals more with the everyday aspects of life related to decisions, relationships, passages to freedom, adventures, search for meaning and purpose, family experiences, and encounters with God rather than movement of one life stage to another. Fear and anxiety may accompany young people in the midst of these turning points. Some examples include the fear of being known, boredom, unforeseen expectations, restrictions, not knowing enough or not being capable, being stereotyped, sharing or explaining one's faith, family impact, and manipulation.[31]

Engaging biblical lament can help spiritual caregivers walk with young people in the midst of their turning points by welcoming the accompanying losses and crises. "By learning to welcome loss and crisis, you will not shy away when youth or their families enter dark times and look to you for spiritual help. Instead, you will be a conduit of God's presence, allowing God to move through you as you listen and seek to understand what support to offer."[32] Lament will enable young people to deal with their own potential changes resulting from these turning points by helping them connect and understand their emotions with their experiences. It offers space for them to reflect on those experiences and see God's role in them. Finally, engaging practices of lament will help young

29. Ibid., 5.

30. Ibid., 10–11.

31. Ibid., 36–38.

32. Ibid., 113.

people to name their fears and anxieties and offer those up to God and share those with friends and adult spiritual caregivers.

Story-telling

Stories can lead us to great adventure; they can also lead us astray. They enable us to make deep human connections by constructing meaning for ourselves and communicate to others in ways that conceal or reveal.[33] When our storytelling is used to develop an identity that solely offers a respectable self-interpretation of ourselves for others, it might not square with the stories that others tell of us. This discrepancy may serve to conceal the truth of reality. "We are in danger of being isolated in our life narrative whenever our storytelling conceals more than it reveals."[34] On the other hand, stories that reveal our true, vulnerable selves can "bond us quickly with strangers or deepen the affection of friends or family."[35] In order to weave together our human narratives with the divine narrative, it is important to connect the stories we tell with the rituals that we enact. Our stories are on a continuum of myth and parable. Mythic stories mediate between irreducible opposites by seeking to resolve contradiction and paradox, whereas parabolic stories challenge our expectations of a world without blemish and creates contradiction in order to reveal a truth otherwise hidden.[36]

Rituals and stories can create religious meaning, particularly when the human and the divine narratives are connected in ways that demonstrate co-authorship.[37] Our storytelling and ritual-making can be transformative for both individuals and communities since these acts point beyond themselves to a larger, transcendent narrative. Ministers can help weave together the di-

33. Anderson and Foley, *Mighty Stories, Dangerous Rituals*, 4.

34. Ibid., 10.

35. Ibid., 10.

36. Ibid., 13–14.

37. Ibid., 43.

vine-human narratives in both worship settings and pastoral care moments. Worship can become boring when it is not attentive to the human story, and pastoral care can become too individualized when it is not connected with the divine story.

Engaging in biblical lament will reveal our true stories, rather than conceal them in ways that isolate ourselves from others. Lament is expressing our true selves and emotions rather than covering them up or denying our experienced reality. By revealing ourselves to God and to friends and family around us, we will not only deepen our relationships but will further our supportive connections to each other as we reveal our struggles, doubts, and confusions. Biblical lament, though it may first appear to be a mythic form of storytelling—ending in praise and thus resolving whatever contradiction and paradox that seemingly exists—is more parabolic in nature. The resolution or praise happens only after the paradoxes, conflicts, struggles, etc. are named. Lament helps young people with their storytelling by encouraging truthtelling and refusing denial of reality.[38] This storytelling can be transformative for them. Lament encourages oppressed voices, whether this is due to external or internal forces, to speak up out of their suffering.[39] As Old Testament scholar Claus Westermann once noted, " . . . lament is the language of suffering; in it suffering is given the dignity of language. It will not stay silent!"[40]

Story-Making

In his book *Hear My Story: Understanding the Cries of Troubled Youth,* Dean Borgman suggests that key tasks of youth ministry include "enabling young people to hear someone else's story [and] empowering young people to tell their own stories and be affirmed . . . We might conclude a definition of youth ministry in terms of empowering young people to become storytellers able to help

38. Hamman, *When Steeples Cry,* 120.

39. O'Conner, *Lamentations and the Tears of the World,* 95.

40. Westermann, *Praise and Lament in the Psalm,* 272.

others and serve the human community."[41] Though this book's audience is primarily intended for those who walk with "troubled youth,"[42] his convictions for story-making and story-telling can be applied to all adolescents. He notes that hearing young people's stories takes time, caring, and patience as we wait for them to feel confident to speak up.[43]

Similarly, Dori Grinenko Baker argues for the importance of story-telling in her book *Doing Girlfriend Theology: God-Talk with Young Women*. She also notes the high level of violence that affects our young people today, particularly since murder and suicide are the second and third leading causes of death among fifteen to twenty-four year olds. Grinenko Baker contends, "Yet there is little outlet in our culture, whether in churches, in families, or in schools, for young women to share their experiences of tragedy or explore their groping efforts to make meaning in the midst of confusing messages."[44] She notes that among predominantly white, middle-class girls there is often a "loss of voice" as they move from childhood into junior high and beyond. Girls begin to play into seemingly conventional gender stereotypes as descriptors of "vivacious," "spunky," and "willful" give way to adjectives such as "nonconfrontational," "nice and kind," and "pleasing."[45]

However, it is through story-telling where young women can ask, "Where is God in this story?" Story-telling is salvation work. She notes, "When we engage in the sharing of stories, we engage in a communal, saving work of reinterpreting our inherited traditions

41. Borgman, *Hear My Story*, 12.

42. For the purposes of Borgman's book *Hear My Story: Understanding the Cries of Troubled Youth*, "troubled youth" are young people who are in imminent danger of inflicting serious injury on themselves or others, primarily those who display suicidal or homicidal behaviors (page 23). He estimates that this comprises nearly 5 percent of US teenagers (page 26). "Youth at risk," on the other hand, is a broader term that includes "those who are in situations or have manifested early behaviors that may only point in the direction of trouble or suggest minor difficulties" (page 23).

43. Borgman, *Hear My Story*, 13.

44. Grinenko Baker, *Doing Girlfriend Theology*, viii.

45. Ibid., 13.

into forms and shapes that make sense in an emerging landscape. By saving our stories, we participate in saving our selves, connecting our lives to the evolving Christian tradition, and engaging with Christ in the ongoing incarnation of God's word in the world."[46] Though this book is primarily intended for those who walk with adolescent girls and young women, the principles and methods can be applied to adolescent boys and young men with relative ease.

Engaging in biblical lament is a form of story-telling and story-making. As young people read the laments of biblical authors and those from other poets and story-tellers, they can begin to better understand contexts involving suffering, loss, and grief. Hearing and reading other people's stories will help to give voice to their own pain and internal grief; it will help them grasp and articulate their own feelings. And just as lament can empower those who may have "lost their voices," it can also remind us of when God too experienced a "loss of voice." The devastation found in Lamentations left God speechless.[47] Knowing this story may allow us to honor other types of non-verbal statements.

Conclusion

The three-step, six-minute, timed-writing prayer exercise is one way to engage biblical lament with young people. This chapter offers both variations of that particular prayer exercise, as well as how lament might be incorporated into other faith practices we engage with young people. Obviously there are many more ideas to be dreamed up than are contained in this chapter and book. Engaging in practices of lament will foster a spirituality with God that is honest, real, and reassuring.

The two youth pastors I interviewed who led their various youth groups in practices of biblical lament are now more equipped to deal with tragedy and situations of grief they encounter with adolescents. Since the onset of this project, disruptive

---

46. Ibid., 32.

47. O'Conner, *Lamentations and the Tears of the World*, 85.

crisis situations have arisen among individual young people in their care. Both shared with me that utilizing biblical lament was one of the first pastoral responses they considered. Below is a portion of an email that I received from one of the youth pastors a few months after she concluded leading her youth in the prayer of lament exercises for this project.

> "So on Monday night, 2 kids from _____ High School died in a car accident. Bible study last night was about mourning and we did the lament exercise. It was so incredibly meaningful for my youth and I think they all valued being led in this type of prayer, where they could write out their thoughts and emotions and share with God. We talked about how Jesus mourned when Lazarus died and we talked about Jesus being the Resurrection and Life—and the promise of eternal life that we have in Jesus, which is why in the beatitudes Jesus says, 'blessed are those who mourn, for they will be comforted.' I just thought I would thank you for the educating you have done which prepared me to lead my youth during this difficult tragedy in their lives. So thank you, Bob. Continue to spread the news of the power of lament in our lives!"

7

Conclusion

HELPING YOUTH GRIEVE: THE Good News of Biblical Lament. The first part of the book's title implies that grief is a common reality. Loss affects youth in a variety of ways, from the mundane to the tragic. Grief and loss are part of life's normal routine; they are not the exception. The last part of the title recognizes that God cares for us—all parts of us! God has been walking with humans in the realities of our life experience since the Garden of Eden. As the relationship between God and God's people continued over time, God has welcomed the honest and raw utterances from a people who God deeply loves.

I am confident that as youth lament, they will grow in their belief and faith in God. At this stage in their life it is important for young people to engage in practices of biblical lament. Increased rates of teenage depression, suicide, eating disorders, cutting, parental divorce, and academic and extracurricular pressures testify to this need. However, every age group has their own particular issues and grievances that should be lamented. Adolescence is not unique among the various age groups needing to lament! What is distinctive, however, are some of the reasons why these young people need to experience God's loving acceptance. One of my hopes for this book is that it can be a source of encouragement for spiritual caregivers of youth, whether you are pastors, parents, teachers, camp personnel, etc., as you lovingly respond to your youth for the world they live in.

Pre-Project Assumptions, Post-Project Learnings

The Christian practice employed in the project described in chapter 3 was a three-step, six-minute, timed-writing prayer exercise of lament. Adolescents wrote their raw emotions to God, their remembrances of a time when God was faithful to them, and their praises to God. Prior to the project, I was convinced that our American society and church knew little about biblical lament. This proved to be true among the settings for this project since the high majority of adolescents indicated they had not previously engaged in such prayers. Churches need to become more aware of and engage in practices of biblical lament for its potential impact on the faith of young people and older adults alike.

Another assumption I had was that there would be differences among early, middle, and late adolescents in how they would engage this prayer exercise. This also proved to be true. Early adolescent prayers were more concrete in dealing with everyday life issues involving family, friends, and school and were less abstract than middle and late adolescents. Middle adolescents also lamented the mundane aspects of life, but they also wrote about abstract issues of morality, personal sin, and human suffering. Late adolescents yearned for deeper intimacy with God and direction in life.

A third observation I had expected to see was differences between males and females. I thought boys would be more resistant to writing and voluntarily turning in their laments compared to girls, and that the content and topics of the actual prayers would be significantly different. However, the results of this study demonstrated no measured distinctions between the genders. In talking with the two youth pastors, they noted that individual personalities of youth served as a better indicator for the depth of serious engagement with this practice than gender.

Fourth, I had assumed that most young people would find the timed-writing exercise helpful and comfortable. This too was true, but I did not foresee reading the high percentage of comments testifying that the most enjoyable part of this prayer was "expressing their emotions to God." I believe this offers compelling evidence that young people need to release pent up emotions and are yearning to reach out to a listening ear, whether that be from God or other people. Adolescents need spiritually mature adult caregivers to walk with them in a way that authentically enables them to face and deal with their inner emotions in positive ways. Engaging practices of biblical lament is one approach.

Finally, I had expected some resistance by young people regarding the practice of arguing and venting explicit emotions against God. Overall, there was not much evidence of this. In fact, most young people found this to be a beneficial way of praying. The discomfort that did occur among a small percentage of participants generally centered on issues of writing out their prayers and not always knowing what to pray about. I had also imagined that there would be a significant number of young people stating that their friends, parents, and other adults they knew would not be comfortable with this practice. However, the overwhelming majority thought that they would be comfortable engaging it and that it would be good for them to release their own emotions and connect with God in this way.

The findings of this project furthers my belief that engaging in practices of biblical lament is needed by adolescents, as well as by adults. The time is ripe to proactively lead young people in such ways.

Adolescent Pastoral Care

Churches today might engage people with biblical lament during times of major or disruptive crisis, as in the death of a parent or loved one and any other significant tragedy. However, I believe it is equally important to nurture young people through rehearsals of biblical lament due to the normal, mundane aspects of loss encountered in everyday life. The overwhelming response of young people who took part in this project affirmed the opportunity to express their emotions to God.

Young people, I believe, are desperately looking for safe places to release their inner tensions brought on by normal everyday life happenings. Rather than turning to destructive practices of cutting, eating disorders, alcohol and drug abuse, lament can be a constructive outlet. It will build upon the resilience of young people and lead them into a lifestyle of hope. However, it will take informed and courageous spiritual adult leaders to help forge the way for adolescents. And, will challenge us as caregivers to face our own unresolved pain and scars.

Adolescent Faith Formation

The National Study of Youth and Religion found that adolescents are inarticulate about their faith beliefs. Practices of biblical lament will enable young people to communicate their obscure emotions, murky frustrations, and ambiguous questions of doubt related to areas of faith. Lament offers a framework for which to surface those vague and ambivalent stirrings. At a time of intense communal loss and faith crisis, Lamentations was birthed. The acrostic and alphabetic devices used by these ancient composers model a structured way to deal with the chaos of unstructured pain, doubt, and confusion. The Psalms invite people to a balanced, holistic spiritual walk with God as they engage all one hundred and fifty prayers, with lament being the largest category.

Theologically, this type of prayer exercise offers an understanding of God to young people as one who is ever-listening and receptive to their honest selves. At a time when many young people search to belong and seek out meaningful relationships, lament cultivates an image of a God who is loving, accepting, and caring. If adults are abandoning young people because of physical absence or by spurring on over-involvement in extracurricular activities, lament will enable adolescents to know God as a faithful, ever-present being, even when they may not feel it.

Psalms and Lamentations show that lament fosters truth-telling and encourages a "spirituality of protest" as opposed to passive acceptance of suffering. Jesus models this way of praying as he hung on the cross and recited parts of Psalm 22, "My God, my God, why have you forsaken me?" As adolescents grow in maturity and life experience, they can know that God is not one who revels in the suffering of humanity, but one who allows people to cry out in ways that compels God to listen and see the present pain. God is then called to act or respond to those who suffer in accordance with God's steadfast love.

The two youth pastors highly affirmed this way of praying because it points our words to God and eventually may lead to praise of God. This makes lament distinguishable from mere complaint. Complaining with no hope of anything ever being resolved or ever accepting the consequences of our actions enable a shallow, immature faith to persist. Lament, however, challenges us to action through our words and possible deeds.

Practicing Lament

I have personally led this timed-writing prayer exercise of lament with people of all ages for over a decade. The findings of this project suggest that this is an effective way to introduce young people to the practice of biblical lament. They value the time to express their emotions to God and are empowered to articulate their questions, doubts, fears, and frustrations of their lives. It also directs them to God and offers a structural format for personal, guided reflection. There are adaptations to this particular prayer exercise that youth leaders will want to consider for both individual and corporate settings, as offered in chapter 6. Lament could also be incorporated into the regular rituals, rites of passage, turning points, story-telling, and story-making practices of the church.

I also offer two words of caution. First, with any of these practices, youth leaders should never strong-arm young people to participate in or share their prayers of lament to others if they are not willing to do so. Forcing them will deteriorate the safe, nurturing space needed and may generate inauthentic prayers. Second, given the National Study of Youth and Religion's description that youth today narrowly view God as a therapeutic being, is there for people only when they call out to God, and expect God to answer their needs in order to make them happy, this relatively short practice could foster a sense of "MTD therapy" if not appropriately carried out. It is vital that spiritual caregivers lead youth through this prayer exercise in ways that encourage authentic expressions of prayer and in ways that remain true to God's character. If youth engage this three-step prayer as some sort of "magic formula" to get what they want or to avoid the pain or emotion of step 1 by rushing to praise, then this will go against the transformative power of biblical lament. And though the actual lament Psalms vary in length, step 1 often occupies more verses than the other components of lament. This too speaks to the importance of spending adequate time naming our hurt and loss. Afterall, some laments "stay in the pit."

A Final Prayer

In the Introduction, I identified several people in my life who have enabled me to express my emotions to God and to myself. My father modeled to me and granted me permission that "it's okay to cry." My former volunteer youth worker simply held me and offered no words as I grieved over the casket of my friend. Engaging practices of biblical lament will not only empower our young people to carry out truth-telling, help them deal with those parts that they wish to deny, articulate a view of God that yearns to be with us, and facilitate mourning of the major and everyday losses they experience, it will also encourage adult spiritual caregivers to more confidently walk with young people through the challenges and joys of life. Engaging practices of biblical lament will call us to attend to our own areas of grief and loss so that we can be better and more authentic spiritual caregivers.

There was a particular time in my life when I was going through some struggles that lasted a couple of years. I was in my mid-thirties. Some of it was related to adjusting to the role of being a parent of two young children; some of it had to do with changes in my job, as well as some tensions in the church where my wife pastored; and some of it was connected to a brother being diagnosed with terminal cancer, a parent facing Alzheimer's Disease, and a mother-in-law experiencing significant health challenges. Simply put, there were a number of "heavy things" going on in my life. But in this time I also experienced a certain type of "dryness" within my own spiritual faith. It was difficult for me to adequately explain what all was going on inside of me to my spiritual director, yet it seemed there was no real "energetic life" or joy in my inner faith. I did not believe that I committed any particular sin that made me feel this way, nor did I doubt God's presence with me in life. In many ways, I felt as close to God as I ever did. Yet, "dryness" is what I experienced. My "spiritual feelings" were flat-lined.

Month after month as I talked with my spiritual director, I expressed my "gratefulness" for knowing about biblical lament. For me, faith in God is more than just a "feeling." Faith is living out realizing God is with us, even when the not-so-fun-that-are-beyond-our-control-realities visit our lives. Lament allowed me to know that it was okay to hang out in step 1 and not rush myself to steps 2 and 3. Psalm 88 started in the pit and ended in the pit. So why would there not be such times in life for many of us? There was no use in trying to climb out of a dry pit that was not climbable at that time. It was enough to know that God was with me in the pit.

Biblical lament reassured me of God's love for me even when I did not "feel" it. It gave me permission to cry out my raw emotions, questions, and frustrations to God. And, those prayers were good enough for a period of time in my life. Eventually after about one and a half years that "dryness" left and a certain kind of joy was rekindled in my faith experience again. But had I not known about biblical lament or grieved through previous deep hurts in my life, I am not sure where I would have come out in regards to my faith. Would I have abandoned it? I do not know, but I do know that knowing about and engaging in practices of biblical lament helped to keep my faith centered on God.

I pray that when those dark and challenging times envelope young people, they will have already known about and encountered the God of lament.

Bibliography

Anderson, Herbert, and Edward Foley. *Mighty Stories, Dangerous Rituals: Weaving Together the Human and the Divine.* San Francisco: Jossey-Bass, 2001.

Arnett, Jeffrey. *Emerging Adulthood: The Winding Road from the Late Teens through the Twenties.* New York: Oxford University Press, 2004.

Atkinson, Harley. *Ministry with Youth in Crisis.* Birmingham, AL: Religious Education, 1997.

Balcomb, Marcey and Kevin Witt. *Twists of Faith: Ministry with Youth at Turning Points.* Nashville: Discipleship Resources, 1999.

Bass, Dorothy, and Don Richter, eds. *Way to Live: Christian Practices for Teens.* Nashville: Upper Room Books, 2002.

Billman, Kathleen, and Daniel Migliore. *Rachel's Cry: Prayer of Lament and Rebirth of Hope.* Cleveland: United Church, 1999.

Borgman, Dean. *Hear My Story: Understanding the Cries of Troubled Youth.* Peabody, MA: Hendrickson, 2003.

Brown, Sally, and Patrick Miller. "Introduction." In *Lament: Reclaiming Practices in Pulpit, Pew and Public Square,* edited by Sally Brown and Patrick Miller, xiii–xix. Louisville: Westminster John Knox, 2005.

Brueggemann, Walter. "Foreword." In *Psalms of Lament,* by Ann Weems, ix–xiv. Louisville: Westminster John Knox, 1995.

———. *The Message of the Psalms: A Theological Commentary.* Minneapolis: Augsburg, 1984.

———. *Spirituality of the Psalms.* Minneapolis: Fortress, 2002.

Cannister, Mark. "Youth Ministry's Historical Context: The Education and Evangelism of Young People." In *Starting Right: Thinking Theologically About Youth Ministry,* edited by Kenda Creasy Dean, et al., 77–90. Grand Rapids, MI: Zondervan, 2001.

Carotta, Michael. *Sometimes We Wrestle, Sometimes We Dance: Embracing the Spiritual Growth of Adolescents.* Orlando: Harcourt Religious, 2002.

Centers for Disease Control and Prevention. "Alcohol and Other Drug Use." 12 June 2014. Web. 15 Dec. 2014. http://www.cdc.gov/healthyyouth/alcoholdrug/index.htm.

————. "Suicide Among Youth." 1 Aug. 2013. Web. 7 Dec. 2014. http://www.cdc.gov/healthcommunication/toolstemplates/entertainmented/tips/suicideyouth.html.

————. "Suicide Prevention: Youth Suicide." 9 January 2014. Web. 15 Dec. 2014. http://www.cdc.gov/violenceprevention/pub/youth_suicide.html#2.

Clark, Chap. "The Changing Face of Adolescence: A Theological View of Human Development." In *Starting Right: Thinking Theologically About Youth Ministry*, edited by Kenda Creasy Dean, et al., 41–61. Grand Rapids, MI: Zondervan, 2001.

————. *Hurt 2.0: Inside the World of Today's Teenagers*. Grand Rapids, MI: Baker Academic, 2011.

Cooper-White, Pamela. "Opening the Eyes: Understanding the Impact of Trauma on Development." In *In Her Own Time: Women and Developmental Issues in Pastoral Care*, edited by Jeanne Stevenson-Moessner, 87–101. Minneapolis: Fortress, 2000.

Couture, Pamela. *Seeing Children, Seeing God: A Practical Theology of Children and Poverty*. Nashville: Abingdon, 2000.

Creasy Dean, Kenda. *Practicing Passion: Youth and the Quest for a Passionate Church*. Grand Rapids, MI: Eerdmans, 2004.

Daloz Parks, Sharon. *Big Questions, Worthy Dreams: Mentoring Emerging Adults in Their Search for Meaning, Purpose, and Faith*. San Francisco: Jossey-Bass, 2011.

Dobbs-Allsopp, F. W. *Lamentations: Interpretation, a Bible Commentary for Teaching and Preaching*. Louisville: John Knox, 2002.

Duff, Nancy J. "Recovering Lamentation as a Practice in the Church." In *Lament: Reclaiming Practices in Pulpit, Pew, and Public Square*, edited by Sally Brown and Patrick Miller, 3–14. Louisville: Westminster John Knox, 2005.

Dunn, Richard. *Shaping the Spiritual Life of Students: A Guide for Youth Workers, Pastors, Teachers, and Campus Ministers*. Downers Grove, IL: InterVarsity, 2001.

Dykstra, Craig. *Counseling Troubled Youth*. Louisville: Westminster John Knox, 1997.

———— and Dorothy Bass. "A Theological Understanding of Christian Practices." In *Practicing Theology: Beliefs and Practices in Christian Life*, edited by Miroslav Volf and Dorothy Bass, 13–32. Grand Rapids, MI: Eerdmans, 2002.

Dykstra, Robert C. "Rending the Curtain: Lament as an Act of Vulnerable Aggression." In *Lament: Reclaiming Practices in Pulpit, Pew and Public Square*, edited by Sally Brown and Patrick Miller, 59–69. Louisville: Westminster John Knox, 2005.

Elkind, David. *The Hurried Child: Growing Up Too Fast Too Soon*. Cambridge, MA: Da Capo, 2001.

Grimes, Ronald. *Deeply Into the Bone: Re-Inventing Rites of Passage*. Los Angeles: University of California Press, 2000.

Grinenko Baker, Dori. *Doing Girlfriend Theology: God-Talk with Young Women.* Cleveland: The Pilgrim Press, 2005.

Hamman, Jaco. *When Steeples Cry: Leading Congregations Through Loss and Change.* Cleveland: The Pilgrim Press, 2005.

Hogue, David. *Remembering the Future, Imagining the Past: Story, Ritual, and the Human Brain.* Cleveland: The Pilgrim Press, 2003.

Jinkins, Michael. *In the House of the Lord: Inhabiting the World of the Psalms.* Collegeville, MN: The Liturgical Press, 1998.

Johnson, William Stacy. "Jesus' Cry, God's Cry, and Ours." In *Lament: Reclaiming Practices in Pulpit, Pew and Public Square,* edited by Sally Brown and Patrick Miller, 80–94. Louisville: Westminster John Knox, 2005.

Klaassen, Walter, editor. *Anabaptism in Outline: Selected Primary Sources.* Scottdale, PA: Herald, 1981.

Loewen, Harry, and Steven Nolt. *Through Fire and Water: An Overview of Mennonite History.* Scottdale, PA: Herald, 1996.

Lytch, Carol. *Choosing Church: What Makes a Difference for Teens.* Louisville: Westminster John Knox, 2004.

Miller, Alice. *The Drama of the Gifted Child: The Search for the True Self.* New York: HarperCollins, 1997.

Miller, Patrick. "Heaven's Prisoners: The Lament as Christian Prayer." In *Lament: Reclaiming Practices in Pulpit, Pew and Public Square,* edited by Sally Brown and Patrick Miller, 15–26. Louisville: Westminster John Knox, 2005.

Molitor, Brian. *Boy's Passage, Man's Journey.* Lynwood, WA: Emerald Books, 2004.

National Study of Youth and Religion. "Research Purpose." Web. 17 Dec. 2014. http://youthandreligion.nd.edu/research-purpose.

O'Conner, Kathleen. *Lamentations and the Tears of the World.* Maryknoll, NY: Orbis Books, 2002.

Oswald, Roy. *Transforming Rituals: Daily Practices for Changing Lives.* Herndon, VA: Alban Institute, 1999.

Parrott III, Les. *Helping the Struggling Adolescent: A Guide to Thirty-Six Common Problems for Counselors, Pastors, and Youth Workers.* Grand Rapids, MI: Zondervan, 2000.

Robbins, Duffy. *This Way to Youth Ministry: An Introduction to the Adventure.* Grand Rapids, MI: Zondervan, 2004.

Rowatt, G. Wade, Jr. *Adolescents in Crisis: A Guide for Parents, Teachers, Ministers, and Counselors.* Louisville: Westminster John Knox, 2001.

Smith, Christian. *Soul Searching: The Religious and Spiritual Lives of American Teenagers.* New York: Oxford University Press, 2005.

Snyder, C. Arnold. *Anabaptist History and Theology: An Introduction.* Kitchener, ON: Pandora, 1995.

Somé, Malidoma Patrice. *Ritual: Power, Healing, and Community.* New York: Penguin Compass, 1993.

Weaver, Andrew, et al. *Counseling Troubled Teens and Their Families: A Handbook for Pastors and Youth Workers*. Nashville: Abingdon, 1999.

Weems, Ann. *Psalms of Lament*. Louisville: Westminster John Knox, 1995.

Westermann, Claus. *Praise and Lament in the Psalms*. 2nd ed. Atlanta: John Knox, 1981.

White David. *Practicing Discernment with Youth: A Transformative Youth Ministry Approach*. Cleveland: The Pilgrim Press, 2002.